A BIBLIOGRAPHY
OF THE PERIODICAL LITERATURE
ON THE ACTS OF THE APOSTLES
1962-1984

SUPPLEMENTS TO
NOVUM TESTAMENTUM

VOLUME LVIII

LEIDEN — E. J. BRILL — 1986

A BIBLIOGRAPHY
OF THE PERIODICAL LITERATURE
ON THE ACTS OF THE APOSTLES
1962-1984

BY

WATSON E. MILLS

LEIDEN — E. J. BRILL — 1986

ISBN 90 04 08130 5

TABLE OF CONTENTS

Preface

The idea for this bibliography arose while I was working on another project that required intensive use of periodical material relating to the Acts of the Apostles. In course of that work I made extensive use of A. J. Mattill and Mary Benford Mattill, *A Classified Bibliography of the Literature on the Acts of the Apostles* (Brill, 1966). This excellent volume contained references to literature published before 1962. In the course of completion of my project I amassed considerable periodical material published *after* that time; I have since supplemented these citations, seeking to be as comprehensive as possible. In most cases, I have attempted to include articles *not* included in Mattill regardless of the date of publication, though their list is virtually definitive for the period covered.

The attempt is made here to update the listing of materials that appeared in Mattill; but there are important differences to note. (1) The Mattill volume included references to books and monographs while the present volume includes *only* periodical materials. (2) The arrangement here is alphabetical by author while the Mattill volume was arranged topically.

Another work that covers some of the same materials is Günter Wagner's *An Exegetical Bibliography of the New Testament*. This definitive work was first published on reference cards, but more recently in casebound edition (Mercer University Press): Vol. I, Matthew and Mark (1983); Vol. II, Luke and Acts (1985); Vol. III, Johannine Writings (1986); others to come. As in the case of Mattill, this work contains references to books and monographs as well as periodical literature. Again, the layout is different from that of the present work since references are displayed by relating each to one or more specific scriptural citations. Here I have chosen to provide several indexes which I hope will provide easy access to the materials included.

In course of preparing this bibliography I have utilized the resources of the following libraries: University of Chicago; Duke University; University of Edinburgh; Emory University; Graduate Theological Union; Harvard University; University of Louvain; Princeton Theological Seminary; Southern Baptist Theological Seminary; Southern Methodist University; Southwestern Theological Seminary; Union Theological Seminary, Richmond; Yale University.

I wish to thank my colleagues, Rollin S. Armour and Robert G. Bratcher, who proofread the entire manuscript and offered many helpful suggestions for its improvement. Also, I acknowledge the contribution of my administrative assistant, Irene Pace, for assisting in the preparation of all drafts of these materials. Her patience and attention to detail is only surpassed by her willingness to work long hours.

Also, I thank the administration of Mercer University for funds that enabled me to visit the above mentioned libraries.

Watson E. Mills
Mercer University
July 1986

Abbreviations

BZNW Beihefte zur Zeitschrift für die Neuentestamentliche Wissenschaft

BEvT Beiträge zur Evangelischen Theologie

BibO Bibbia e Oriente

BiKi Bibel und Kirche

BibLeb Bibel und Leben

BiLi Bibel und Liturgie

Bhash Biblebhashyam

BTS Bible et Terre Sainte

BibVie Bible et Vie Chrétienne

BibTo Bible Today

BiTr Bible Translator

BibFe Biblia y Fe

Bib Biblica

BibRv Biblia Revuo

BA Biblical Archaeologist

BiR Biblical Research

BTh Biblical Theology

BibTB Biblical Theology Bulletin

BETL Bibliotheca Ephemeridum Theologicarum Lovaniensium

BS Bibliotheca Sacra

BTSt Biblisch-Theologische Studien

BiBe Biblische Beiträge

BN Biblische Notizen

BZ Biblische Zeitschrift

Bij Bijdragen

BogS Bogoslovska Smotra

BBB Bonner Biblische Beiträge

BTB Bulletin de Théologie Biblique

BCPE Bulletin du Centre Protestant d'Études

BASP Bulletin of the American Society of Papyrologists

BETS Bulletin of the Evangelical Theological Society
BJRL Bulletin of the John Rylands Library

CahC Cahiers du Cercle
CTJ Calvin Theological Journal
CanJT Canadian Journal of Theology
Cath Catholica
CBQ Catholic Biblical Quarterly
ChrTo Christianity Today
Chr Christus
Ch Churchman
ChQR Church Quarterly Review
Cist Revista Monástica Cistercium
CC La Civiltà Cattolica
CB Classical Bulletin
ClM Clergy Monthly
CRev Clergy Review
Col Collationes, Vlaams Tijdschrift voor Theologie en Pastoraal
ColT Collectanea Theologica
Com Communio
CV Communio Viatorum
Conc Concilium
CJ Concordia Journal
CTM Concordia Theological Monthly
CNeo Conniectanea Neotestamentica
CCr Cross and Crown
CuT Cuadernos Teológicos
CuBi Cultura Bíblica
CuTM Currents in Theology and Mission

DTT Dansk Teologisk Tidsskrift

JAC Jahrbuch für Antike und Christentum
JOAI Jahreshefte des Österreichischen Archäologischen Instituts
Je Jeevadhara
JQR Jewish Quarterly Review
JTC Journal for Theology and the Church
JSNT Journal for the Study of the New Testament
JBL Journal of Biblical Literature
JJS Journal of Jewish Studies
JRPR Journal of Religion and Psychical Research
JRH Journal of Religious History
JAAR Journal of the American Academy of Religion
JTS Journal of Theological Studies
JETS Journal of the Evangelical Theological Society
Jud Judaica
Judm Judaism

K Kairos
KB Katechetische Blätter
KS Kator Shin

La Laurentianum
LT Laval Théologique et Philosophique
LS Lebendige Seelsorge
LD Lectio Divina
LTQ Lexington Theological Quarterly
LB Linguistica Biblica
LL Living Light
LQHR London Quarterly and Holborn Review
LVie Lumière et Vie
LV Lumen Vitae

Mar Marburger Theologische Studien
MHC Mélanges Henri Cazellas

MT   Melita Theologica
Misc   Miscellanea Franciscana

Miss   Missiology

Mu   Muséon

NGTT   Nederduitse Gereformeerde Teologiese Tydskrif

NTT   Nederlands Theologisch Tijdschrift

Neo   Neotestamentica

NTS   New Testament Studies

NTTid   Norsk Teologisk Tidsskrift

NRT   Nouvelle Revue Théologique

NT   Novum Testamentum

OC   One in Christ

OBO   Orbis Biblicus et Orientalis

OCh   Oriens Christianus

OCP   Orientalia Christiana Periodica

Or   Orientierung

OS   Ostkirchliche Studien

OT   Oud-Testamentiese Werkgemeenskap in Suid-Afrika

PC   Palestra del Clero

Para   Paraclete

PL   Paroise et Liturgie

PSV   Paròla, Spirito e Vita

PV   Parole di Vita

PRS   Perspectives in Religious Studies

Pn   Pneuma

PIB   Pontificio Instituto Biblico

PL   Positions Luthériennes

PIBA   Proceedings of the Irish Biblical Association

QD   Quaestiones Disputatae

RBL	Ruch Biblijny i Liturgiczny
SacD	Sacra Doctrina
Sac	Sacerdos
Sal	Salesianum
Salm	Salmanticensis
SalT	Sal Terrae
SE	Science et Esprit
SJT	Scottish Journal of Theology
Sc	Scripture
SB	Scripture Bulletin
ScuC	Scuola Cattolica
SelT	Selecciones de Libros/Teologia
Sem	Semeia
SémB	Sémiotique et Bible
Ser	Servitium
SWJT	Southwestern Journal of Theology
SIC	Strumento Internazionale Communio
StB	Studia Biblica
SBT	Studia Biblica et Theologica
SEv	Studia Evangelium
ST	Studia Theologica
STV	Studia Theologica Varsaviensia
STE	Studi di Teologia Evangelico
SNTU	Studien zum Neuen Testament und seiner Umwelt
SJLA	Studies in Judaism in Late Antiquity
SR	Studies in Religion
SBFLA	Studii Biblici Franciscani Liber Annuus
STS	Studii Theologico Seria
Stud	Studium
SVTQ	St. Vladimir's Theological Quarterly
Sum	Summarium

SEÅ Svensk Exegetisk Årsbok

TJT Taiwan Journal of Theology

Tel Telema

Teo Teologia

TA Teologinen Aikakauskirja

TS Terre Sainte

TI Text and Interpretations

TK Texte und Kontexte

TU Texte und Untersuchungen

TVia Theologia Viatorum

TG Theologie der Gegenwart

TGl Theologie und Glaube

TP Theologie und Philosophie

TL Theologische Literaturzeitung

TQ Theologische Quartalschrift

TR Theologische Rundschau

TVer Theologische Versuche

TZ Theologische Zeitschrift

TPQ Theologisch Praktische Quartalschrift

T Theology

TD Theology Digest

TsTK Tidsskrift for Teologi og Kirke

TTZ Trierer Theologische Zeitschrift

TJ Trinity Journal

TB Tyndale Bulletin

USQR Union Seminary Quarterly Review

VD Verbum domini

VF Verkündigung und Forschung

Vid Vidyajyoti

VSS Vie Spirituelle Supplément

VC Vigiliae Christianae

VE Vox Evangelica

VR Vox Reformata

WTJ Westminster Theological Journal

WM Wissenschaftliche Monographien zum Alten und Neuen Testament

WWo Word and World

W Worship

WD Wort und Dienst

WWa Wort und Wahrheit

ZZ Zeichen der Zeit

ZDP Zeitschrift des Deutschen Palästinavereins

ZNW Zeitschrift für die Neutestamentliche Wissenschaft

ZKT Zeitschrift für Katholische Theologie

ZRGG Zeitschrift für Religions- und Geistesgeschichte

ZTK Zeitschrift für Theologie und Kirche

ALPHABETICALLY BY JOURNAL ABBREVIATION

ABR Australian Biblical Review

AC Analecta Cracoviensia

ACQ American Church Quarterly

ACR Australasian Catholic Record

AHC Annuarium Historiae Conciliorum

AKap Ateneum Kaplanskie

AmiCl Ami du Clergé

AnBib Analecta Biblica

Ang Angelicum

ANQ Andover Newton Quarterly

AntAb Antike und Abendland

Anton Antonianum

Arch Archéologia

AS Asiatische Studien (Études Asiatiques)

AsbS Asbury Seminarian

AssS Assemblées du Seigneur

ASTI Annual of the Swedish Theological Institute

ATB Ashland Theological Bulletin

ATR Anglican Theological Review

Aug Augustinianum

AUSS Andrews University Seminary Studies

AuV Abraham unser Vater

BA Biblical Archaeologist

BASP Bulletin of the American Society of Papyrologists

BBB Bonner Biblische Beiträge

BCPE Bulletin du Centre Protestant d'Études

BETL Bibliotheca Ephemeridum Theologicarum Lovaniensium

BEvT Beiträge zur Evangelischen Theologie

Bhash Biblebhashyam

Bib	Biblica
BiBe	Biblische Beiträge
BibFe	Biblia y Fe
BibLeb	Bibel und Leben
BibO	Bibbia e Oriente
BibRv	Biblia Revuo
BibTB	Biblical Theology Bulletin
BibTo	Bible Today
BibVie	Bible et Vie Chrétienne
Bij	Bijdragen
BiKi	Bibel und Kirche
BiLi	Bibel und Liturgie
BiR	Biblical Research
BiTr	Bible Translator
BJRL	Bulletin of the John Rylands Library
BN	Biblische Notizen
BogS	Bogoslovska Smotra
BS	Bibliotheca Sacra
BTB	Bulletin de Théologie Biblique
BTh	Biblical Theology
BTS	Bible et Terre Sainte
BTSt	Biblisch-Theologische Studien
BZ	Biblische Zeitschrift
BZNW	Beihefte zur Zeitschrift für die Neuentestamentliche Wissenschaft
CahC	Cahiers du Cercle
CanJT	Canadian Journal of Theology
Cath	Catholica
CB	Classical Bulletin
CBQ	Catholic Biblical Quarterly
CC	La Civiltà Cattolica

GeL Geist und Leben
GNT Gnosis und Neuen Testament
GOTR Greek Orthodox Theological Review
GRBS Greek, Roman and Byzantine Studies
GTJ Grace Theological Journal
GTT Gereformeerd Theologisch Tijdschrift

HB Homiletica en Biblica
Hel Helmantica
HJ Hibbert Journal
HK Herder Korrespondenz
HLV Heilige Land in Vergangenheit und Gegenwart
Hok Hokhma
HTR Harvard Theological Review
HTS Hervormde Teologiese Studies

IBS Irish Biblical Studies
IEJ Israel Exploration Quarterly
IJT Indian Journal of Theology
IKZ Internationale Katholische Zeitschrift/Communio
Int Interpretation
Ir Irénikon
ITQ Irish Theological Quarterly
ITS Indian Theological Studies

JAAR Journal of the American Academy of Religion
JAC Jahrbuch für Antike und Christentum
JBL Journal of Biblical Literature
Je Jeevadhara
JETS Journal of the Evangelical Theological Society
JJS Journal of Jewish Studies
JOAI Jahreshefte des Österreichischen Archäologischen Instituts
JQR Jewish Quarterly Review

JRH Journal of Religious History
JRPR Journal of Religion and Psychical Research
JSNT Journal for the Study of the New Testament
JTC Journal for Theology and the Church
JTS Journal of Theological Studies
Jud Judaica
Judm Judaism

K Kairos
KB Katechetische Blätter
KS Kator Shin

La Laurentianum
LB Linguistica Biblica
LD Lectio Divina
LL Living Light
LQHR London Quarterly and Holborn Review
LS Lebendige Seelsorge
LT Laval Théologique et Philosophique
LTQ Lexington Theological Quarterly
LV Lumen Vitae
LVie Lumière et View

Mar Marburger Theologische Studien
MHC Mélanges Henri Cazellas
Misc Miscellanea Franciscana
Miss Missiology
MT Melita Theologica
Mu Muséon

Neo Neotestamentica
NGTT Nederuitse Gereformeerde Teologiese Tydskrif
NRT Nouvelle Revue Théologique

SBFLA Studii Biblici Franciscani Liber Annuus
SBT Studia Biblica et Theologica
Sc Scripture
ScuC Scuola Cattolica
SE Science et Esprit
SEv Studia Evangelium
SEÅ Svensk Exegetisk Årsbok
SelT Selecciones de Libros/Teologia
Sem Semeia
SémB Sémiotique et Bible
Ser Servitium
SIC Strumento Internazionale Communio
SJLA Studies in Judaism in Late Antiquity
SJT Scottish Journal of Theology
SNTU Studien zum Neuen Testament und seiner Umwelt
SR Studies in Religion
ST Studia Theologica
StB Studia Biblica
STE Studi di Teologia Evangelico
STS Studii Theologico Seria
Stud Studium
STV Studia Theologica Varsaviensia
Sum Summarium
SVTQ St. Vladimir's Theological Quarterly
SWJT Southwestern Journal of Theology

T Theology
TA Teologinen Aikakauskirja
TB Tyndale Bulletin
TD Theology Digest
Tel Telema
Teo Teologia

TG Theologie der Gegenwart

TGl Theologie und Glaube

TI Text and Interpretations

TJ Trinity Journal

TJT Taiwan Journal of Theology

TK Texte und Kontexte

TL Theologische Literaturzeitung

TP Theologie und Philosophie

TPQ Theologisch Praktische Quartalschrift

TQ Theologische Quartalschrift

TR Theologische Rundschau

TS Terre Sainte

TsTK Tidsskrift for Teologi og Kirke

TTZ Trierer Theologische Zeitschrift

TU Texte und Untersuchungen

TVer Theologische Versuche

TVia Theologia Viatorum

TZ Theologische Zeitschrift

USQR Union Seminary Quarterly Review

VC Vigiliae Christianae

VD Verbum Domini

VE Vox Evangelica

VF Verkündigung und Forschung

Vid Vidyajyoti

VR Vox Reformata

VSS Vie Spirituelle Supplément

W Worship

WD Wort und Dienst

WM Wissenschaftliche Monographien zum Alten und Neuen Testament

WTJ Westminster Theological Journal
WWA Wort und Wahrheit
WWO Word and World

ZDP Zeitschrift des Deutschen Palästinavereins
ZKT Zeitschrift für Katholische Theologie
ZNW Zeitschrift für die Neutestamentliche Wissenschaft
ZRGG Zeitschrift für Religions- und Geistesgeschichte
ZTK Zeitschrift für Theologie und Kirche
ZZ Zeichen der Zeit

The Bibliography

001 Abri, J. "The Theological Meaning of Pentecost," *KS* 4/1 (1965): 133-51 [*see also* 011, 012, 025, 201, 230, 239, 247, 266, 279, 322, 346, 437, 483, 552, 665, 672, 705, 722, 808, 892, 932, 973, 975].

002 Acworth, A. "Where Was St. Paul Shipwrecked? A Re-examination of the Evidence," *JTS* 24/1 (1973): 190-93.

003 Adinolfi, Marco. " 'Obbedire a Dio piuttosto che algi uomni.' La comunità cristiana e il sinedrio in Atti 4,1-31; 5,17-42," *RBib* 27/1-2 (1979): 69-93 [*see also* 021, 133, 296, 308, 355, 445, 512, 551, 569, 632, 703, 777, 801, 810, 897, 927, 928].

004 _____. "San Paolo á Pozzuoli (Atti 28, 13b-14b)," *RBib* 8/3 (1960): 206-24 [*see also* 005, 118, 392, 501, 669, 734].

005 _____. "San Paolo e le Auorità Romane negli Atti degli Apostoli," *Anton* 53/3-4 (1978): 452-70 [*see also* 004, 118, 392, 501, 669, 734].

006 Adler, Nikolaus. "Die Kirche baute sich auf . . . und mehrte sich durch den Beistand nach der Apostelgeschichte," *BiKi* 21/2 (1966): 48-51 [*see also* 042, 064, 076, 078, 084, 100, 126, 128, 148, 189, 195, 196, 277, 309, 312, 315, 319, 320, 322, 327, 371, 372, 387, 403, 439, 459, 462, 475, 482, 519, 522, 528, 532, 541, 549, 574, 586, 590, 609, 611, 614, 623, 632, 643, 692, 699, 709, 737, 755, 759, 772, 783, 784, 808, 817, 830, 864, 867, 872, 891, 894, 898, 900, 913, 917, 919, 934, 939, 944, 960, 964, 974].

007 Agouridis, S. "Confrontation with Hellenistic-era Magic in Acts," *DBM* 5 (1977): 119-35 [*see also* 530].

008 _____. "Hē antimetōpisē tēs Mageias tōn Hēllenistikōn chronōn apo to Biblio tōn Praxeōn tōn Apostolōn," *DBM* 5/2-3 (1977-1978): 119-35 [*see also* 146, 249, 981].

009 _____. "Die Stellung der Apostelgeschichte zur Magie der hellenistischen Zeit," *DBM* 5/2-3 (1978): 119-35.

010 Alldrit, N. "La Kristologia de la Parolado de Sankta Petro en Agoj 10:34-44," *BibRv* 7 (1966): 28-31 [*see also* 016, 374, 423, 466, 482, 488, 502, 533, 555, 581, 626, 629, 677, 792, 863, 900, 953].

011 Alvarez de Linera, A. "Glosólalo y Intéprete," *Estudios Biblicos*, 9 (1950): 193-208 [*see also* 001, 012, 025, 201, 230, 239, 247, 266, 279, 322, 346, 437, 483, 552, 665, 722, 808, 932, 973, 975].

012 Amoit, F. "Glossolalie," *Cath* 5 (1962): 67-69.

013 Anon. "New Testament Studies: 3. The Brother of the Lord," *HJ* 61/1 (1962): 44-45 [*see also* 106, 448, 942].

014 Argyle, A. W. "Acts xix. 20," *ET* 75/5 (1964): 151.

015 _____. "The Greek of Luke and Acts," *NTS* 20 (1974): 441-45.

016 Atienza, J. Colmenero. "Hechos 7,17-43 y las corrientes cristológicas dentro de la primitiva comunidad cristiana," *EB* 33/1 (1974): 31-62 [*see also* 010, 374, 423, 466, 482, 488, 502, 533, 555, 581, 626, 629, 677, 792, 863, 900, 953].

017 Auffret, P. "Essai sur la structure littéraire du discours d'Athènes (Ac xvii 23-31)," *Bib* 59/11 (1978): 979-99 [*see also* 020, 086, 091, 132, 276, 394, 509, 604, 635, 680, 725, 852, 980].

018 de Azevedo, M. Cagiano. "La prima compagna di scavi a Malta della Missione Archeologia Italiana e le memorie paoline," *BibO* 6/3 (1964): 135-39.

019 Bagatti, B. "Nuove testimonianze sul luogo della lapidazione di S. Stefano," *Anton* 49/4 (1974): 527-32.

020 Bahnsen, G. L. "The Encounter of Jerusalem with Athens," *ATB* 13/1 (1980): 4-40 [*see also* 017, 086, 091, 132, 276, 394, 509, 604, 635, 680, 725, 852, 980].

021 Balagué, M. "Hechos 7, 17-43 y las corrientes cristológicas dentro de la primitiva communidad cristiana," *EB* 33 (1974): 33-67 [*see also* 003, 133, 296, 308, 355, 445, 512, 551, 569, 632, 703, 777, 801, 810, 897, 927, 928].

022 Ballarini, T. "ARCHEGOS (*Atti* 3:15, 5:31; *Ebr.* 2:10, 12:2) autore o condottiero?" *SacD* 16/63-64 (1971): 535-51.

023 _____. "Collegialità della Chiesa in Atti e in Galati," *BibO* 6/6 (1964): 255-62.

024 Bamberger, B. J. "The Sadducees and the Belief in Angels," *JBL* 82/4 (1963): 433-35 [*see also* 055, 058, 077, 142, 168, 223, 334, 343, 363, 386, 458, 462, 506, 508, 609, 675, 678, 683, 756, 763, 803, 832, 862, 950].

025 Banks, R. J. and G. N. Moon, "Speaking in Tongues: A Survey of New Testament Evidence," *Ch* 80 (1966): 278-94 [*see also* 001, 011, 012, 201, 230, 239, 247, 266, 279, 322, 346, 437, 483, 552, 665, 722, 808, 932, 973, 975].

026 Barnard, L. W. "Saint Stephen and Early Alexandrian Christianity," *NTS* 7/1 (1960): 31-45 [*see also* 016, 059, 063, 075, 122, 129, 180, 188, 311, 323, 327, 397, 464, 486, 487, 504, 526, 571, 690, 707, 716, 717, 757, 769, 820, 837, 847, 848, 849, 881, 886, 912, 928, 950, 958].

027 Barnes, Timothy D. "An Apostle on Trial," *JTS* 20/2 (1969): 407-19 [*see also* 063, 112, 138, 282].

028 Barrett, C. Kingsley. "Acts and the Pauline Corpus," *ET* 88/1 (1976): 2-5 [*see also* 182, 280, 283, 366, 696, 734, 783, 788, 789].

029 _____. "Apostles in Council and in Conflict," *ABR* 31 (1983): 14-32 [*see also* 178, 234, 245, 246, 251, 281, 408, 414, 461, 617, 662, 711, 713, 758, 847, 857].

030 _____. "Salvation Proclaimed: XII. Acts 4:8-12," *ET* 94/3 (1982): 68-71 [*see also* 216, 234, 240, 465, 560].

031 Barrosse, T. "Religious Community and the Primitive Church," *RevRel* 25/6 (1966): 971-85 [*see also* 056, 191, 228, 229, 238, 264, 302, 316, 455].

032 Barthes, Roland. "L'Analyse Structurale du Récit. A propos d'Actes 10-11," *RSR* 58/1 (1970): 17-37 [*see also* 573].

033 Bates, W. H. "A Note on Acts 13:39," *TU* 112 (1973): 8-10.

034 Bauernfeind, O. "Tradition und Komposition in dem Apokatastasisspruch Apg 3,20f," *AuV* (1963): 13-23.

035 Baumbach, G. "Die Anfänge der Kirchwerdung im Urchristentum," *K* 24/1-2 (1982): 17-30 [*see also* 100, 148, 167, 178, 232, 323, 372, 503, 504, 564, 609, 661, 739, 760, 777, 784, 812, 850, 854, 869, 870, 890, 895, 941, 971, 984, 987].

036 Baus, K. "Le origini. Inizi e affermazione di Milane. I Padri e il monachesimo eremitico (I-IV sec.)," *VC* 15 (1978): 166.

037 Bazán, F. García. "En torno a Hechos 8,4-24. Milagro y magia entre los gnósticos," *RBib* 40/1 (1978): 27-38 [*see also* 063, 109, 174, 208, 270, 602, 603, 681, 690, 800].

038 Beardslee, W. A. "The Casting of Lots at Qumran and in the Book of Acts," *NT* 4/4 (1960): 245-52 [*see also* 187, 278, 425, 537, 654, 787, 963, 970].

039 Becq, J. "Paul rencontre les païens de Lystres," *BTS* 135 (1971): 16 [*see also* 047, 282, 288, 525, 938].

040 Benoit, Pierre. "La mort de Judas," *ExT* 1 (1961): 340-59.

041 _____. "Remarques sur les 'sommaires' des Actes II, IV et V," *ExT* 2 (1961): 181-92.

042 Berchmans, J. "Anointed with Holy Spirit and Power," *Je* 8/45 (1978): 201-17 [*see also* 006, 064, 076, 078, 084, 100, 126, 128, 148, 189, 195, 196, 277, 309, 312, 315, 319, 320, 322, 327, 371, 372, 387, 403, 439, 459, 462, 475, 482, 519, 522, 528, 532, 541, 549, 574, 586, 590, 609, 611, 614, 623, 632, 643, 692, 699, 709, 737, 755, 759, 772, 783, 784, 808, 817, 830, 864, 867, 872, 891, 894, 898, 900, 913, 917, 919, 934, 939, 944, 960, 964, 974].

043 van Bergen, P. "L'Epître de la Pentecôte (Acts 2,1-14)," *PL* 4 (1961): 253-62 [*see also* 001, 076, 077, 078, 088, 101, 110, 121, 126, 154, 178, 190, 221, 239, 240, 242, 300, 340, 370, 465, 493, 512, 528, 541, 577, 590, 611, 613, 624, 644, 665, 687, 692, 737, 787, 806, 808, 812, 813, 817, 862, 888, 900, 902, 930, 939, 960, 964, 975].

044 Best, E. "Acts xiii. 1-3," *JTS* 11/2 (1960): 344-48 [*see also* 089, 180, 252, 288, 645, 653, 661, 708, 795, 815, 877, 893, 942, 980].

045 Betori, G. "L'Antico Testamento negli Atti. Stato della ricerca e spunti di riflessione," *RBib* 32/4 (1984): 211-36.

046 _____. "Persiguitati a causa del nome. Strutture dei racconti di persecuzione in Atti 1,12-8,4," *AnBib* 97 (1981): 240.

047 Beutler, Johannes. "Die paulinische Heidenmission am Vorabend des Apostelkonzils. Zur Redaktionsgeschichte von Apg 14,1-20," *TP* 43/3 (1968): 360-83 [*see also* 039, 282, 288, 525, 938].

048 Beyschlag, K. "Zur Simon-Magua-Frage," *ZTK* 78 (1971): 395-426 [*see also* 008, 037, 174, 365, 670, 799, 868].

049 Bieder, W. "Die Königsherrschaft Gottes in der Apostelgeschichte des Lukas," *EM* 104/1 (1960): 2-8.

050 ———. "Der Petrusschatten, Apg. 5,15," *TZ* 16/5 (1960): 407-409 [*see also* 107, 162, 176, 181, 219, 245, 250, 252, 328, 414, 498, 640, 645, 658, 672, 711, 785, 787, 815, 942, 964, 965].

051 Bishop, E. F. F. "Guide to Those Who Arrested Jesus," *EQ* 40/1 (1968): 41-42.

052 Black, Mark. "Paul and Roman Law in Acts," *RQ* 24/4 (1981): 209-18.

053 Blair, Edward P. "Paul's Call to the Gentile Mission," *BiR* 10 (1965): 19-33 [*see also* 245, 358, 427, 429, 430, 545].

054 Blanquart, F. "Le discernement au temps de jeunes communautés," *NRT* 104/4 (1982): 577-84.

055 Blenkinsopp, J. "The Bible and the People: The Ascension as Mystery of Salvation," *CRev* 50/5 (1965): 369-74 [*see also* 154, 175, 207, 210, 269, 274, 335, 368, 369, 462, 506, 508, 531, 536, 539, 540, 612, 614, 793, 827, 959, 977].

056 Blevins, W. L. "The Early Church: Acts 1-5," *REx* 71/4 (1974): 463-74 [*see also* 031, 191, 228, 229, 238, 264, 302, 316, 455].

057 Blinzler, J. "Rechtsgeschichtliches zur Hinrichtung des Zebedäiden Jakobus (Apg xii 2)," *NT* 5/2-3 (1962): 191-206 [*see also* 687].

058 Boers, H. W. "Psalm 16 and the Historical Origin of the Christian Faith," *ZNW* 60/1-2 (1969): 105-10 [*see also* 024, 055, 077, 142, 168, 223, 334, 343, 363, 386, 458, 462, 506, 508, 609, 675, 678, 683, 756, 763, 803, 832, 862, 950].

059 Boismard, M.-É. "Le martyre d'Étienne. Actes 6,8-8,2," *RSR* 69/2 (1981): 181-94 [*see also* 057, 461, 689, 885, 914].

060 Boman, T. "Das textkritische Problem des sogenannten Apos-
teldekrets," *NT* 7/1 (1964): 26-36 [*see also* 237, 358, 367,
377, 378, 460, 490, 511, 537, 578, 698, 789, 827, 862, 896,
908, 910, 914, 926, 955, 970, 977].

061 Bori, Pier Cesare. "Chiesa primitiva, Atti 2:4," *RTP* 110 (1978):
306.

062 Borse, U. "Kompositionsgeschichtliche Beobachtungen zum
Apostelkonzil," *BBB* 53 (1980): 195-212.

063 _____. "Der Rahmentext im Umkreis der Stephanusge-
schichte (Apg 6,1-11,26)," *BibLeb* 14/3 (1973): 187-204 [*see
also* 027, 112, 138, 282].

064 Bourassa, F. "L'Esprit Saint 'communion' du Pére ed du Fils,"
SE 30/1 (1978): 5-37 [*see also* 006, 042, 076, 078, 084, 100,
126, 128, 148, 189, 195, 196, 277, 309, 312, 315, 319, 320,
322, 327, 371, 372, 387, 403, 439, 459, 462, 475, 482, 519,
522, 528, 532, 541, 549, 574, 586, 590, 609, 611, 614, 623,
632, 643, 692, 699, 709, 737, 755, 759, 772, 783, 784, 808,
817, 830, 864, 867, 872, 891, 894, 898, 900, 913, 917, 919,
934, 939, 944, 960, 964, 974].

065 Bouyer, Louis. "Von der Judischen zur christlichen Liturgie,"
Com 7 (1978): 509-19.

066 Bovon, François. "Luc: portrait et projet," *LVie* 30/153-54
(1981): 9-18.

067 _____. "L'origine des recits concernant les apôtres," *RTP*
17/5 (1967): 345-50 [*see also* 082, 303, 304, 341, 357, 409,
576].

068 _____. "Tradition et rédaction en Actes 10,1-11,18," *TZ*
26 (1970): 22-45.

069 Bowers, W. P. "Paul's Route Through Mysia: A Note on Acts
16:8," *JTS* 30/2 (1979): 507-11 [*see also* 047, 151, 155, 156,
163, 166, 280, 329, 476, 615, 841, 949, 984].

070 Bowker, J. W. "Speeches in Acts: A Study in Proem and Ye-
lammedenu Form," *NTS* 14/1 (1967/1968): 96-111 [*see also*
096, 115, 193, 199, 326, 497, 554, 647, 839, 846, 867, 921,
968].

071 Bratcher, Robert G. "ἀκούω in Acts 9:7 and 23:9," *ET* 71/8
(1960): 243-45.

072 Braun, M. A. "James' Use of Amos at the Jerusalem Council: Steps Toward a Possible Solution of the Textual and Theological Problems," *JETS* 20/2 (1977): 113-21 [*see also* 687].

073 Brinkman, J. A. "The Literary Background of the 'Catalogue of the Nations' (Acts 2,9-11)" *CBQ* 25/3 (1963): 418-27.

074 Brock, S. P. "ΒΑΡΝΑΒΑΣ: ΥΙΟΣ ΠΑΡΑΚΛΗΣΕΩΣ," *JTS* 25 (1974): 93-98.

075 Brodie, T. L. "The Accusing and Stoning of Naboth (1 Kgs 21:8-13) as One Component of the Stephen Text (Acts 6:9-14; 7:58a)," *CBQ* 45/3 (1983): 417-32 [*see also* 016, 026, 059, 063, 122, 129, 180, 188, 311, 323, 327, 397, 464, 486, 487, 504, 526, 571, 690, 707, 716, 717, 757, 769, 820, 837, 847, 848, 849, 881, 886, 912, 928, 950, 958].

076 Broer, Ingo. "Der Geist und die Gemeinde. Zur Auslegung der lukanischen Pfingstgeschichte (Apg 2,1-13)," *BibLeb* 13/4 (1972): 261-83 [*see also* 006, 042, 064, 078, 084, 100, 126, 128, 148, 189, 195, 196, 277, 309, 312, 315, 319, 320, 322, 327, 371, 372, 387, 403, 439, 459, 462, 475, 482, 519, 522, 528, 532, 541, 549, 574, 586, 590, 609, 611, 614, 623, 632, 643, 692, 699, 709, 737, 755, 759, 772, 783, 784, 808, 817, 830, 864, 867, 872, 891, 894, 898, 900, 913, 917, 919, 934, 939, 944, 960, 964, 974].

077 Brown, S. "Easter and Pentecost: A Biblical Reflection on Their Relationship," *W* 46/5 (1972): 277-86 [*see also* 001, 043, 076, 078, 088, 101, 110, 121, 126, 154, 178, 190, 221, 239, 240, 242, 300, 340, 370, 465, 493, 512, 528, 541, 577, 590, 611, 613, 624, 644, 665, 687, 692, 737, 787, 806, 808, 812, 813, 817, 862, 888, 900, 902, 930, 939, 960, 964, 975].

078 _____. " 'Water-Baptism' and 'Spirit-Baptism' in Luke-Acts," *ATR* 59/2 (1977): 135-51 [*see also* 006, 042, 064, 076, 084, 100, 126, 128, 148, 189, 195, 196, 277, 309, 312, 315, 319, 320, 322, 327, 371, 372, 387, 403, 439, 459, 462, 475, 482, 519, 522, 528, 532, 541, 549, 574, 586, 590, 609, 611, 614, 623, 632, 643, 692, 699, 709, 737, 755, 759, 772, 783, 784, 808, 817, 830, 864, 867, 872, 891, 894, 898, 900, 913, 917, 919, 934, 939, 944, 960, 964, 974].

079 Brox, Norbert. "Nikolaos und Nikolaiten," *VC* 19/1 (1965): 23-30.

080 Bruce, F. F. _____. "The Acts of the Apostles Today," *BJRL* 65/1 (1982): 36-56.

081 _____. "Apollos in the New Testament," *EP* 57/3-4 (1975): 354-66.

082 _____. "Commentaries on Acts," *EpR* 8/3 (1981): 82-87 [*see also* 067, 303, 304, 341, 357, 409, 576].

083 _____. "The Full Name of the Procurator Felix," *JSNT* 1 (1978): 33-36 [*see also* 236].

084 _____. "The Holy Spirit in the Acts of the Apostles," *Int* 27/2 (1973): 166-83 [*see also* 006, 042, 064, 076, 078, 100, 126, 128, 148, 189, 195, 196, 277, 309, 312, 315, 319, 320, 322, 327, 371, 372, 387, 403, 439, 459, 462, 475, 482, 519, 522, 528, 532, 541, 549, 574, 586, 590, 609, 611, 614, 623, 632, 643, 692, 699, 709, 737, 755, 759, 772, 783, 784, 808, 817, 830, 864, 867, 872, 891, 894, 898, 900, 913, 917, 919, 934, 939, 944, 960, 964, 974].

085 _____. "Is the Paul of Acts the Real Paul?" *BJRL* 58/2 (1976): 282-305.

086 _____. "Paul and the Athenians," *ET* 88/1 (1976): 8-12 [*see also* 017, 020, 091, 132, 276, 394, 509, 604, 635, 680, 725, 852, 980].

087 _____. "St. Paul in Macedonia," *BJRL* 61/2 (1979): 337-54 [*see also* 151].

088 Brunot, Amédée. "La Pentecôte d'Éphèse," *BTS* 144 (1972): 4-5 [*see also* 390, 436, 451, 467, 674, 700, 868, 924].

089 Bruzzone, G. B. "Il dissenso tra Paolo e Barnaba in Atti 15,39," *EB* 35 (1976): 121 [*see also* 044, 180, 252, 288, 645, 653, 661, 708, 795, 815, 877, 893, 942, 980].

090 Budesheim, T. L. "Paul's *Abschiedsrede* in the Acts of the Apostles," *HTR* 69/1-2 (1976): 9-30 [*see also* 243, 448, 700].

091 Bultmann, R. "Sermon sur le descours de Paul à Áreopage," *VSS* 114 (1975): 303-13 [*see also* 017, 020, 086, 132, 276, 394, 509, 604, 635, 680, 725, 852, 980].

092 van de Bunt-van den Hoek. "Aristobulos, Acts, Theophilus, Clement. Making Use of Aratus' Phainomena: A Peregrination," *Bij* 41/3 (1980): 290-99 [*see also* 582, 619, 730].

093 Burchard, C. "Der dreizehnte Zeuge: Traditions–und kompositionsgeschichtliche Untersuchungen zu Lukas' Darstellung der Frühzeit des Paulus," *FRL* 103/52 (1970): 3463 [*see also* 364, 765].

094 _____. "Ei nach einem Ausdruck des Wissins oder Nichtwissens Joh 9:25, Act 19:2, I Cor 1:16, 7:16," *ZNW* 52/1-2 (1961): 73-82.

095 _____. "Paulus in der Apostelgeschichte," *TL* 100/12 (1975): 881-95.

096 Burini, C. "Gli studi dal 1950 ad oggi sul numero e sulla classificazione dei discorsi degli 'Atti degli Apostoli'—un contributo d'individuazione," *La* 15/3 (1974): 349-65 [*see also* 070, 115, 193, 199, 326, 497, 554, 647, 839, 846, 867, 921, 968].

097 _____. "Gli studi dal 1950 ad oggi sul numero e sulla classificazione dei discorsi degli 'Atti degli Apostoli.' Un contributo d'individuazione (II)" *La* 16/1-2 (1975): 191-207.

098 Calloud, J. "Paul devant l'Aréopage d'Athènes. Actes 17,16-34," *RSR* 69/2 (1981): 209-48 [*see also* 086, 091, 217, 218, 243, 431, 432, 554, 678, 725, 852].

099 Calvino, R. "Cristiani a Puteoli nell'anno 61. Riflessioni zu sull'importanza della notizia concisa degli 'Atti' (28,13b-14a) e risposta all'interrogativo sulle testimonianze monumentali coeve," *RivAC* 56/3-4 (1980): 323-30.

100 Cambier, J. "Le Voyage de S. Paul à Jérusalem en Act. ix. 26ss. et le Schéma Missionnaire Théologique de S. Luc," *NTS* 8/3 (1962): 249-57 [*see also* 006, 042, 064, 076, 078, 084, 126, 128, 148, 189, 195, 196, 277, 309, 312, 315, 319, 320, 322, 327, 371, 372, 387, 403, 439, 459, 462, 475, 482, 519, 522, 528, 532, 541, 549, 574, 586, 590, 609, 611, 614, 623, 632, 643, 692, 699, 709, 737, 755, 759, 772, 783, 784, 808, 817, 830, 864, 867, 872, 891, 894, 898, 900, 913, 917, 919, 934, 939, 944, 960, 964, 974].

101 Cantinat, J. "La Pentecôte," *BibVie* 86 (1969): 57-69 [*see also* 001, 043, 076, 077, 078, 088, 110, 121, 126, 154, 178, 190, 221, 239, 240, 242, 300, 340, 370, 465, 493, 512, 528, 541, 577, 590, 611, 613, 624, 644, 665, 687, 692, 737, 787, 806, 808, 812, 813, 817, 862, 888, 900, 902, 930, 939, 960, 964, 975].

102 Capper, B. J. "The Interpretation of Acts 5:4," *JSNT* 19 (1983): 117-31 [*see also* 172, 549, 611, 962].

103 Carrez, Maurice. "L'appel de Paul a Cesar (Ac 25,11): La double appartenance, juive et chrétienne, de la première Église d'après le livre des Actes," *MHC* (1981): 503-10 [*see also* 158, 903].

104 _____. "Présence at fonctionnement de l'Ancien Testament dans l'annonce de l'Évangile," *RSR* 63 (1975): 325-42.

105 Casalegno, A. "Il discorso di Mileto (*Atti* 20,17-38)," *RBib* 25/1 (1977): 29-58.

106 Catchpole, D. R. "Paul, James and the Apostolic Decree," *NTS* 23/4 (1977): 428-44 [*see also* 129, 184, 201, 435, 454, 498, 527, 554, 601, 701, 895].

107 Catrice, P. "De judéo-christianisme à l'Église de tous les peuples," *BibVie* 79 (1968): 20-30 [*see also* 050, 162, 176, 181, 219, 245, 250, 252, 328, 414, 498, 640, 645, 658, 672, 711, 785, 787, 815, 942, 964, 965].

108 _____. "Réflexions missionnaires sur la vision de Saint Pierre à Joppé. Du judéo-christianisme à l'Église de tous les peuples," *BibVie* 79 (1968): 30-39 [*see also* 129, 250, 360, 542, 573, 587, 658, 688, 838, 873].

109 Charbel, A. "La fontana di Filippo di Ain el-Haniyah (Act 8,26-40)," *TS* 53 (1978): 150-54 [*see also* 037, 063, 174, 208, 270, 602, 603, 681, 690, 800].

110 Charnov, B. H. "Shavout, 'Matan Torah,' and the Triennial Cycle," *Judm* 28 (1974): 332-36 [*see also* 001, 043, 076, 077, 078, 088, 101, 121, 126, 154, 178, 190, 221, 239, 240, 242, 300, 340, 370, 465, 493, 512, 528, 541, 577, 590, 611, 613, 624, 644, 665, 687, 692, 737, 787, 806, 808, 812, 813, 817, 862, 888, 900, 902, 930, 939, 960, 964, 975].

111 Cheetham, F. P. "Acts ii. 47: ἔχοντες χάριν πρὸς ὅλον τὸν λαόν," *ET* 74/7 (1963): 214-15.

112 Ch'en Chia-shih. "The Role of Paul in the Acts of the Apostles," *TJT* 1 (1979): 109-24 [*see also* 027, 063, 138, 282].

113 Chenu, Marie-Dominique. "Au temps des Ordres Mendiants," *LVie* 30/153-54 (1981): 143-49.

114 Cherry, R. S. "Acts xvi. 14f," *ET* 75/4 (1964): 114 [*see also* 760].

115 Chmiel, J. "Tradycja apostolska a redakcja Eukasza w Dziejach Apostolskich," *AC* 8 (1976): 125-31 [*see also* 070, 096, 193, 199, 326, 497, 554, 647, 839, 846, 867, 921, 968].

116 Cieslik, P. "Kerygmat o Jezusie z Nazaretu w kazaniach misyjnych Dziejow Apostolskich," *RBL* 34/2 (1981): 113-19.

117 Cipriani, Settimio. "La preghiera negli Atti degli Apostoli," *BibO* 13/1 (1971): 27-41.

118 Clark, D. J. "What Went Overboard First?" *BiTr* 26/1 (1975): 144-46 [*see also* 004, 005, 392, 501, 669, 734].

119 Clavel-Lévéque, M. and R. Nouailhat. "Ouverture et compromis. Les actes de apôtres, résponse idéologique aux nouvelles réalitiés impériales," *LV* 30/153-54 (1981): 35-58.

120 Clifton, J. "Shaping the Kerygma: A Study of Acts," *LL* 10/4 (1973): 522-30 [*see also* 342, 453, 518, 619, 852, 952].

121 Cocchini, F. "L'evoluzione storico-religiosa della festa de Pentecoste," *RBib* 25 (1977): 297-326 [*see also* 001, 043, 076, 077, 078, 088, 101, 110, 126, 154, 178, 190, 221, 239, 240, 242, 300, 340, 370, 465, 493, 512, 528, 541, 577, 590, 611, 613, 624, 644, 665, 687, 692, 737, 787, 806, 808, 812, 813, 817, 862, 888, 900, 902, 930, 939, 960, 964, 975].

122 Coggins, R. J. "The Samaritans and Acts," *NTS* 28/3 (1982): 423-34 [*see also* 129].

123 Colaclides, P. "Acts 17,28A and Bacchae 506," *VC* 27/3 (1973): 161-64.

124 Colin, J. "Une affaire de tapage nocturne devant l'empereur Auguste," *RPH* 44/1 (1966): 21-24.

125 Collange, Jean-Francois. "De Jesus de Nazareth a Paul de Tarse," *LVie* 139 (1978): 87-95.

126 Collins, Joseph D. "Discovering the Meaning of Pentecost," *Sc* 20/51 (1968): 73-79 [*see also* 006, 042, 064, 076, 078, 084, 100, 128, 148, 189, 195, 196, 277, 309, 312, 315, 319, 320, 322, 327, 371, 372, 387, 403, 439, 459, 462, 475, 482, 519, 522, 528, 532, 541, 549, 574, 586, 590, 609, 611, 614, 623, 632, 643, 692, 699, 709, 737, 755, 759, 772, 783, 784, 808, 817, 830, 864, 867, 872, 891, 894, 898, 900, 913, 917, 919, 934, 939, 944, 960, 964, 974].

127 Combet-Galland, Anne-Etienne et Corinna. "Actes 4,32-5,11," *ETR* 52/4 (1977): 548-53.

128 Combrink, H. J. B. "Parresia in Handelinge," *NGTT* 16/1 (1975): 56-63 [*see also* 006, 042, 064, 076, 078, 084, 100, 126, 148, 189, 195, 196, 277, 309, 312, 315, 319, 320, 322, 327, 371, 372, 387, 403, 439, 459, 462, 475, 482, 519, 522, 528, 532, 541, 549, 574, 586, 590, 609, 611, 614, 623, 632, 643, 692, 699, 709, 737, 755, 759, 772, 783, 784, 808, 817, 830, 864, 867, 872, 891, 894, 898, 900, 913, 917, 919, 934, 939, 944, 960, 964, 974].

129 Comiskey, J. P. "All the Families of the Earth Will Be Blessed," *BibTo* 83 (1976): 753-62 [*see also* 106, 184, 201, 435, 454, 498, 527, 554, 601, 701, 895].

130 Conde, A. Linage. "¿Vida Monastica en las Acta Apostolorum?" *TU* 112/6 (1973): 321-27.

131 Conzelmann, H. "Geschichte, Geschichtsbild und Geschichtsdarstellung bei Lukas," *TL* 85 (1960): 241-50.

132 _____. "Die Rede des Paulus auf dem Areopag," *BEvT* 65 (1974): 91-105 [*see also* 017, 020, 086, 091, 276, 394, 509, 604, 635, 680, 725, 852, 980].

133 Coppens, J. "La koinônia dans l'Église primitive," *ETL* 46/1 (1970): 116-21 [*see also* 003, 021, 296, 308, 355, 445, 512, 551, 569, 632, 703, 777, 801, 810, 897, 927, 928].

134 Corbin, M. "Connais-tu ce que tu lis? Une lecture d'Actes 8,v.26 à 40," *Chr* 24/93 (1977): 73-85 [*see also* 306, 343, 625].

135 Corell, J. "Actos 10,36," *EF* 76/1 (1975): 101-13.

136 Cothenet, E. "Mission et missions," *DS* 10 (1979): 1349-70 [*see also* 149, 200, 295, 359, 518, 522, 538, 558, 591, 646, 683, 703, 848, 905, 961].

137 Coune, M. "Sauves au nom de Jesus (Ac 4,8-12)," *AssS* 12 (1964): 14-27.

138 Cox, D. "Paul Before the Sanhedrin: Acts 22:30-23:11," *SBFLA* 21 (1971): 54-75 [*see also* 027, 063, 112, 282, 402].

139 Crehan, J. H. "The Confirmation of the Ethiopian Eunuch (Acts 8:39)," *OCP* 195 (1974): 187-95 [*see also* 129, 134, 230, 270, 306, 602, 603, 622, 681]

140 _____. "The Purpose of Luke in Acts," *SEv* 11 (1963): 345-68 [*see also* 157, 556, 592].

141 Croatto, J. Severino. "El Demonio: La Muerte de un Simbolo," *RBib* 40/169 (1978): 147-52.

142 Crumbach, K. H. "Auferstehungszeugnis," *GeL* 48/2 (1975): 81-84 [*see also* 024, 055, 058, 077, 168, 223, 334, 343, 363, 386, 458, 462, 506, 508, 609, 675, 678, 683, 756, 763, 803, 832, 862, 950].

143 Cullmann, O. "Courants multiples dans la communauté primitive. A propos du martyre de Jacques fils de Zébédée," *RSR* 60/1 (1972): 55-68.

144 Culpepper, R. A. "Paul's Mission to the Gentile World: Acts 13-19," *REx* 71/4 (1974): 487-97 [*see also* 363, 382, 427, 449, 524, 538, 683, 701, 774, 782, 935, 944, 969].

145 Dahl, Nils A. "The Origin of the Earliest Prologues to the Pauline Letters," *Sem* 12 (1978): 234-77.

146 Daniel, Constantin. "Un Essénien mentionné dans les Actes des Apôtres: Barjésu," *Mu* 84/3-4 (1971): 455-76 [*see also* 008, 249, 981].

147 _____. "O importanta mentionara a Esenienilor facuta de Sfintul Apostol Pavel (Ein wichtiger Hinweis auf die Essener bei Paulus)," *STS* 29/1-2 (1977): 148-59.

148 Dasiewicz, J. "Jeruzalem—miejscem zeslania Ducha Swietego (Lk 24,49)(Dz 1,4). (Jerusalem—lieu de la descente du Saint Espirit Luc 24,49. Acts 1,4)," *RTK* 23 (1976): 85-96 [*see also* 006, 042, 064, 076, 078, 084, 100, 126, 128, 189, 195, 196, 277, 309, 312, 315, 319, 320, 322, 327, 371, 372, 387, 403, 439, 459, 462, 475, 482, 519, 522, 528, 532, 541, 549, 574, 586, 590, 609, 611, 614, 623, 632, 643, 692, 699, 709, 737, 755, 759, 772, 783, 784, 808, 817, 830, 864, 867, 872, 891, 894, 898, 900, 913, 917, 919, 934, 939, 944, 960, 964, 974].

149 Dautzenberg, Gerhard. "Der Wandel der Reich-Gottes-Verkundigung in der urchristlichen Mission," *QD* 87 (1979): 11-32 [*see also* 136, 200, 295, 359, 518, 522, 538, 558, 591, 646, 683, 703, 848, 905, 961].

150 Davies, P. "The Ending of Acts," *ET* 94/11 (1983): 334-35.

151 _____. "The Macedonian Scene of Paul's Journeys (Acts 16s et 20)," *BA* 26 (1963): 91-106 [*see also* 047, 069, 155, 156, 163, 166, 280, 329, 476, 615, 841, 949, 984].

152 Davis, J. C. "Another Look at the Relationship Between Baptism and Forgiveness of Sins in Acts 2:38," *RQ* 24/2 (1981): 80-88 [*see also* 196, 270, 315, 324, 448, 488, 603, 673, 669, 817, 907, 974].

153 Decock, P. B. "The Understanding of Isaiah 53:7-8 in Acts 8:32,33," *Neo* 14 (1981): 111-33 [*see also* 803].

154 Delebecque, É. "Ascension et Pentecôte dans les Actes des Apôtres selon le codex Bezae," *RThom* 82/2 (1982): 79-89 [*see also* 055, 175, 207, 210, 269, 274, 335, 368, 369, 462, 506, 508, 531, 536, 539, 540, 612, 614, 793, 827, 959, 977].

155 _____. "La dernière étape du troisième voyage missionnaire de saint Paul selon les deux versions des Actes des Apôtres (21,16-17)," *RTL* 14/4 (1983): 446-55 [*see also* 047, 069, 151, 156, 163, 166, 280, 329, 476, 615, 841, 949, 984].

156 _____. "Les deux versions du voyage de saint Paul de Corinthe à Troas (Ac 20,3-6)," *Bib* 64/4 (1983): 556-64 [*see also* 184, 975].

157 _____. "Les deux prologues des Actes des Apôtres," *RThom* 80/4 (1980): 628-34 [*see also* 140, 556, 592].

158 _____. "L'embarquement de Paul, captif, à Césarée, pour Rome *(Actes des Apôtres, 27,1-2),*" *LT* 39/3 (1983): 295-302 [*see also* 103, 903].

159 _____. "L'hellenisme de la 'relative complexe' dans le Nouveau Testament at principalement chez saint Luc," *Bib* 62 (1981): 232-35 [*see also* 171, 837].

160 _____. "De Lystres à Philippes (Ac 16) avec le codex Bezae," *Bib* 63/3 (1982): 395-405 [*see also* 162, 166, 377, 553, 695, 714, 909].

161 _____"La mésaventure des fils de Scévas selon ses deux versions (Actes 19, 13-20)," *RSCPhilT* 66/2 (1982): 225-32.

162 _____. "La montée de Pierre de Césarée à Jérusalem selon le *Codex Bezae* au chapitre 11 des *Actes des Apôtres,*" *ETL* 58/1 (1982): 106-10 [*see also* 160, 166, 377, 553, 695, 714, 909].

163 _____. "Paul à Thessalonique et à Bérée selon le texte occidental des Actes (XVII,4-15)," *RThom* 82/4 (1982): 605-15 [*see also* 047, 069, 151, 155, 156, 166, 280, 329, 476, 615, 841, 949, 984].

164 _____. "La révolte des orfèvres à Éphèse et deux versions *(Actes des Apôtres, 19,24-40),*" *RThom* 83/3 (1983): 419-29.

165 _____. "Saint Paul avec ou sans le tribun Lysias en 58 à Césarée (Actes, XXIV,6-8). Texte court ou texte long?" *RThom* 81/3 (1981): 426-34 [*see also* 700].

166 _____. "Saul et Luc avant le premier voyage missionaire. Comparaison des deux versions des *Actes* 11,26-28," *RSPT* 66/4 (1982): 551-59 [*see also* 160, 162, 377, 553, 695, 714, 909].

167 _____. "Trois simples mots, chargés d'une lumière neuve (Actes des Apôtres, II,47b)," *RThom* 80/1 (1980): 75-85 [*see also* 035, 100, 148, 178, 232, 323, 372, 503, 504, 564, 609, 661, 739, 760, 777, 784, 812, 850, 854, 869, 870, 890, 895, 941, 971, 984, 987].

168 Delling, G. "Die Jesusgeschichte in der Verkündigung nach Acta," *NTS* 19/4 (1973): 373-89 [*see also* 024, 055, 058, 077, 142, 223, 334, 343, 363, 386, 458, 462, 506, 508, 609, 675, 678, 683, 756, 763, 803, 832, 862, 950].

169 _____. "Das Letzte Wort der Apostelgeschichte," *NT* 15/3 (1973): 193-204 [*see also* 578, 985].

170 Delobel, Joel. "Commentaar op Hand. 2,1-11/2,42-47/10,10.34a.37-43," *Sac* 45 (1977): 325-27; 287-89; 208-10.

171 Delorme, J. "Les Hellenistes des Actes des Apôtres," *AmiCl* 71 (1961): 445-47 [*see also* 159, 837].

172 Derrett, J. D. M. "Ananias, Sapphira, and the Right of Property," *DR* 89/296 (1971): 225-32 [*see also* 102, 172, 549, 611, 962].

173 _____. "Miscellanea: A Pauline Pun and Judas' Punishment," *ZNW* 72 (1981): 132-33 [*see also* 176, 332, 336, 559, 567, 654, 687, 763].

174 _____. "Simon Magus (Act 8:9-24)," *ZNW* 73/1-2 (1982): 52-68 [*see also* 037, 063, 109, 208, 270, 602, 603, 681, 690, 800].

175 Devor, R. C. "The Ascension of Christ and the Dissension of the Church," *En* 33/4 (1972): 340-58 [*see also* 055, 154, 207, 210, 269, 274, 335, 368, 369, 462, 506, 508, 531, 536, 539, 540, 612, 614, 793, 827, 959, 977].

176 Dietrich, W. "Das Petrusbild der Judas—Tradition in Acts i.15-26," *NTS* 19/4 (1973): 438-52 [*see also* 173, 332, 336, 559, 567, 654, 687, 763].

177 Doble, P. "The Son of Man Saying in Stephen's Witnessing: Acts 6:8-8:2," *NTS* 31/1 (1985): 68-84.

178 Dockx, S. "Chronologie de la vie de Saint Paul, depuis sa conversion jusqu'à son séjour à Rome," *NT* 13/4 (1971): 261-304 [*see also* 035, 100, 148, 167, 232, 323, 372, 503, 504, 564, 609, 661, 739, 760, 777, 784, 812, 850, 854, 869, 870, 890, 895, 941, 971, 984, 987].

179 _____. "Chronologie paulinienne de l'annee de la grande collecte," *RB* 81 (1974): 183-95.

180 ⎯⎯⎯⎯⎯. ''Date de la mort d'Étienne le Protomartyr,'' *Bib* 55/1 (1974): 65-73 [*see also* 044, 089, 252, 288, 645, 653, 661, 708, 795, 815, 877, 893, 942, 980].

181 ⎯⎯⎯⎯⎯. ''Essai de chronologie pétrinienne,'' *RSR* 62/2 (1974): 221-41 [*see also* 050, 107, 162, 176, 219, 245, 250, 252, 328, 414, 498, 640, 645, 658, 672, 711, 785, 787, 815, 942, 964, 965].

182 ⎯⎯⎯⎯⎯. ''Luc a-t-il été le compagnon d'apostolat de Paul?'' *NRT* 103/3 (1981): 385-400 [*see also* 028 280, 283, 366, 734, 783, 788, 789].

183 ⎯⎯⎯⎯⎯. ''L'ordination de Barnabé et de Saul d'après *Actes 13*, 1-3,'' *NRT* 98/3 (1976): 238-58 [*see also* 316].

184 ⎯⎯⎯⎯⎯. ''Silas a-t-il été le compagnon de voyage de Paul d'Antioche à Corinthe?'' *NRT* 104/5 (1982): 749-53 [*see also* 106, 129, 201, 435, 454, 498, 527, 554, 601, 701, 895].

185 Dodd, Charles H. ''La predicazione apostolica e il suo sviluppo,'' *SacD* 24 (1979): 159.

186 Doignon, J. ''Le dialogue de Jesus et de Paul (Actes 9,4-6). Sa 'pointe' dans l'exegese latine la plus ancienne (Hilaire, Ambroise, Augustin),'' *RSPT* 64/4 (1980): 477-89.

187 Domagalski, B. ''Waren die 'Sieben' (Apg 6.1-7) Diakone?'' *BZ* 26/1 (1982): 21-33 [*see also* 038, 278, 425, 537, 654, 787, 963, 970].

188 Donaldson, T. L. ''Moses Typology and the Sectarian Nature of Early Christian Anti-Judaism: A Study in Acts 7,'' *JSNT* 12 (1981): 27-52 [*see also* 016, 026, 059, 063, 075, 122, 129, 180, 311, 323, 327, 397, 464, 486, 487, 504, 526, 571, 690, 707, 716, 717, 757, 769, 820, 837, 847, 848, 849, 881, 886, 912, 928, 950, 958].

189 Dorr, D. ''Great Deeds in Young Churches—the Acts of the Apostles,'' *Fur* 33/10 (1982): 595-600 [*see also* 006, 042, 064, 076, 078, 084, 100, 126, 128, 148, 195, 196, 277, 309, 312, 315, 319, 320, 322, 327, 371, 372, 387, 403, 439, 459, 462, 475, 482, 519, 522, 528, 532, 541, 549, 574, 586, 590, 609, 611, 614, 623, 632, 643, 692, 699, 709, 737, 755, 759, 772, 783, 784, 808, 817, 830, 864, 867, 872, 891, 894, 898, 900, 913, 917, 919, 934, 939, 944, 960, 964, 974].

190 Downes, J. A. "The Feast of Pentecost: Some Meanings of the Festival in the Bible and the Liturgy," *RUO* 34/1 (1964): 62-69 [*see also* 001, 043, 076, 077, 078, 088, 101, 110, 121, 126, 154, 178, 221, 239, 240, 242, 300, 340, 370, 465, 493, 512, 528, 541, 577, 590, 611, 613, 624, 644, 665, 687, 692, 737, 787, 806, 808, 812, 813, 817, 862, 888, 900, 902, 930, 939, 960, 964, 975].

191 Downey, J. "The Early Jerusalem Christians," *BibTo* 91 (1977): 1295-1303 [*see also* 031, 056, 228, 229, 238, 264, 302, 316, 455].

192 Downing, F. G. "Common Ground with Paganism in Luke and in Josephus," *NTS* 28/4 (1982): 546-59 [*see also* 193, 382, 429, 972].

193 _____. "Ethical Pagan Theism and the Speeches in Acts," *NTS* 27/4 (1981): 544-63 [*see also* 192, 382, 429, 972].

194 Drane, J. W. "Simon the Samaritan and the Lucan Concept of Salvation History," *EQ* 47/3 (1975): 131-37 [*see also* 430, 479, 835, 947].

195 Drumwright, H. L., Jr. "The Holy Spirit in the Book of Acts," *SWJT* 17/1 (1974): 3-17 [*see also* 006, 042, 064, 076, 078, 084, 100, 126, 128, 148, 189, 196, 277, 309, 312, 315, 319, 320, 322, 327, 371, 372, 387, 403, 439, 459, 462, 475, 482, 519, 522, 528, 532, 541, 549, 574, 586, 590, 609, 611, 614, 623, 632, 643, 692, 699, 709, 737, 755, 759, 772, 783, 784, 808, 817, 830, 864, 867, 872, 891, 894, 898, 900, 913, 917, 919, 934, 939, 944, 960, 964, 974].

196 D'Souza, A. "The Sermons of Peter in the Acts of the Apostles," *Bhash* 4/2 (1978): 117-30 [*see also* 152, 270, 315, 324, 448, 488, 603, 673, 699, 817, 907, 974].

197 Dubarle, A.-M. "Le discours à l'Aréopage (*Actes* 17,22-31) et son arrièreplan biblique," *RSPT* 57/4 (1973): 576-610.

198 DuBuit, F. M. "L'Église nait," *Évan* 52/4 (1971): 4-60 [*see also* 289, 356, 454, 499].

199 Dudley, M. B. "The Speeches in Acts," *EQ* 50/3 (1978): 147-55 [*see also* 070, 096, 115, 193, 326, 497, 554, 647, 839, 846, 867, 921, 968].

200 Dumais, M. "Le langage de l'Évangélisation, X L'annonce missionnaire en milieu juif (Acts 13,16-41)" *JTS* 29 (1978): 198 [*see also* 136, 149, 295, 359, 518, 522, 538, 558, 591, 646, 683, 703, 848, 905, 961].

201 _____. "Ministères, charismes et Esprit dans l'oeuvre de Luc," *EgT* 9/3 (1978): 413-53 [*see also* 106, 129, 184, 435, 454, 498, 527, 554, 601, 701, 895].

202 _____. "La rencontre de la foi et des cultures," *LV* 30/153-54 (1981): 72-86.

203 Dumont, Enrique. " 'Koinonia' en los primeros capitulos de los Hechos de los Apóstoles," *RBib* 24 (1962): 22-32 [*see also* 133, 569].

204 Dunn, J. D. G. "The Birth of a Metaphor: Baptized in the Spirit (I)," *ET* 89/5 (1978): 134-38 [*see also* 205, 309].

205 _____. "The Birth of a Metaphor: Baptized in the Spirit (II)," *ET* 89/6 (1978): 173-75 [*see also* 204, 309].

206 _____. "Conversion-initiation dans le livre des Actes," *Hok* 5 (1977): 21-35 [*see also* 213, 401, 457, 563, 621, 670, 691, 873, 874, 906].

207 _____. "Demythologizing the Ascension: A Reply to Professor Gooding," *IrBibStud* 3/1 (1981): 15-27 [*see also* 055, 154, 175, 210, 269, 274, 335, 368, 369, 462, 506, 508, 531, 536, 539, 540, 612, 614, 793, 827, 959, 977].

208 _____. "They Believed Philip Preaching (Acts 8:12): A Reply," *IBS* 1 (1979): 177-83 [*see also* 037, 063, 109, 174, 270, 602, 603, 681, 690, 800].

209 _____. "*Aequitas romana*. Notes sur *Actes* 25, 16," *RSR* 49/3 (1961): 354-85 [*see also* 679, 819].

210 _____. " 'Anelēmphthē (Act. i. 2)" *NTS* 8/2 (1962): 154-57 [*see also* 055, 154, 175, 207, 269, 274, 335, 368, 369, 462, 506, 508, 531, 536, 539, 540, 612, 614, 793, 827, 959, 977].

211 _____. "Des Apôtres à la Lumière d'un Texte de Lucien de Samosate," *NT* 21/3 (1979): 220-31.

212 _____. ''L'apôtre comme intermédiaire du salut dans les
     Actes des Apôtres,'' *RTP* 30/4 (1980): 342-58 [*see also* 220,
     345, 723].

213 _____. ''La conversion en los Hechos de los Apóstoles,''
     SelT 8 (1969): 101-108 [*see also* 206, 401, 457, 563, 621,
     670, 691, 873, 874, 906].

214 _____. ''Les descours missionnaires des Actes des
     Apôtres,'' *RB* 69/1 (1962): 37-60.

215 _____. ''La Destinée de Judas prophetisée par David (Actes
     1,16-20),'' *CBQ* 23/1 (1961): 41-51.

216 _____. ''I discorsi di Pietro negli Atti,'' *Misc* 74 (1974): 273-
     93 [*see also* 030, 234, 240, 465, 560].

217 _____. ''Le discours à l'Aréopage (Ac 17,22-31) lieu de
     rencontre entre christianisme et hellénisme,'' *Bib* 60/4 (1979):
     530-46 [*see also* 086, 091, 098, 218, 243, 431, 432, 554,
     678, 725, 852].

218 _____. ''Le Discours de Milet. Testament Pastoral de Saint
     Paul (Actes 20,18-36),'' *LD* 32 (1962): 9-407 [*see also* 086,
     091, 098, 217, 243, 431, 432, 554, 678, 725, 852].

219 _____. ''Les discours de Pierre dans les Actes et le Chapitre
     XXIV de l'évangile de Luc,'' *BETL* 32 (1973): 329-74 [*see
     also* 050, 107, 162, 176, 181, 245, 250, 252, 328, 414, 498,
     640, 645, 658, 672, 711, 785, 787, 815, 942, 964, 965].

220 _____. ''Le douzième apôtre (*Actes* 1,15-26) à propos d'une
     explication récente,'' *BibO* 24/4 (1982): 193-98 [*see also* 212,
     345, 723].

221 _____. ''L'Épître (de la Pentecôte)(Act 2,I-II): La Première
     Pentecôte chrétienne,'' *AssS* 51 (1963): 39-62 [*see also* 001,
     043, 076, 077, 078, 088, 101, 110, 121, 126, 154, 178, 190,
     239, 240, 242, 300, 340, 370, 465, 493, 512, 528, 541, 577,
     590, 611, 613, 624, 644, 665, 687, 692, 737, 787, 806, 808,
     812, 813, 817, 862, 888, 900, 902, 930, 939, 960, 964, 975].

222 _____. ''L'interprétation des psaumes dans les Actes des
     Apôtres,'' *OBO* 4 (1962): 357-88.

223 _____. ''Τὰ ὅσια Δαυίδ, τὰ πιστά (Ac XIII 34 = Is lv
     3)'' *RBib* 68/1 (1961): 91-114 [*see also* 262].

224 _____. "La première organisation des Églises. Ac 14,21-27," *AssS* 26 (1973): 60-66.

225 _____. "La question du plan des Actes des Apôtres à la lumière d'un texte de Lucien de Samosate," *NT* 21/3 (1979): 220-31.

226 _____. "Salvation of the Pagan World," *TD* 10/1 (1962): 14-18 [*see also* 055, 227, 320, 644, 647].

227 _____. "Le Salut des Gentils et la Signification Théologique du Livre des Actes," *NTS* 6 (1959-60): 146f [*see also* 055, 226, 320, 644, 647].

228 _____. "L'union entre les premiers chrétiens dans les Actes des Apôtres," *NRT* 91/101 (1969): 897-915 [*see also* 031, 056, 191, 229, 238, 264, 302, 316, 455].

229 Eckert, J. "La réalisation de la fraternité dans les premieres communautes chrétiennes," *Conc* 150 (1979): 159 [*see also* 031, 056, 191, 228, 238, 264, 302, 316, 455].

230 Edwards, O. C., Jr. "The Exegesis of Acts 8:4-25 and Its Implications for Confirmation and Glossolalia: A Review Article of E. Haenchen's Acts Commentary," *ATR* SS2 (1973): 100-12 [*see also* 001, 011, 012, 025, 201, 239, 247, 266, 279, 322, 346, 437, 483, 552, 665, 722, 808, 932, 973, 975].

231 Elliger, Winfried. "Die Rede des Apostels Paulus auf dem Areopag (Apg 17,16-34)," *DaU* 25/2 (1982): 63-79 [*see also* 091, 098, 132, 197, 286, 394, 509, 518, 577, 635, 725, 728, 730, 852].

232 Elliott, J. K. "Jerusalem in Acts and the Gospels," *NTS* 23/4 (1977): 462-69 [*see also* 035, 100, 148, 167, 178, 323, 372, 503, 504, 564, 609, 661, 739, 760, 777, 784, 812, 850, 854, 869, 870, 890, 895, 941, 971, 984, 987].

233 Ellis, E. E. "Midraschartige Züge in den Reden der Apostelgeschichte," *ZNW* 62/1-2 (1971): 94-104 [*see also* 567, 915].

234 Ellis, I. M. "Codex Bezae at Acts 15," *IBS* 2 (1980): 134-40 [*see also* 029, 178, 245, 251, 281, 408, 414, 461, 617, 662, 711, 713, 758, 847, 857].

235 Emmelius, Johann C. "Tendenzkritik u. Formengeschichte. Der Beitrag Franz Overbecks zur Auslegung der Apostelgeschichte im 19. jh," *TL* 104 (1979): 124-29 [*see also* 888].

236 Enslin, M. S. "Once Again, Luke and Paul," *ZNW* 61/3-4 (1970): 253-71 [*see also* 083].

237 Epp, E. J. "Coptic Manuscript G67 and the Role of Codex Bezae as a Western Witness in Acts," *JBL* 85/2 (1966): 197-212 [*see also* 060, 358, 367, 377, 378, 460, 490, 511, 537, 578, 698, 789, 827, 862, 896, 908, 910, 914, 926, 955, 970, 977].

238 Epp, H. Jenny. "L'éstablissement de l'Église dans le livre des Actes," *AssS* 52 (1965): 29-45 [*see also* 031, 056, 191, 228, 229, 264, 302, 316, 455].

239 Ervin, Howard M. "As the Spirit Gives Utterance," *ChrTo* 13/14 (1969): 623-26 [*see also* 001, 043, 076, 077, 078, 088, 101, 110, 121, 126, 154, 178, 190, 221, 240, 242, 300, 340, 370, 465, 493, 512, 528, 541, 577, 590, 611, 613, 624, 644, 665, 687, 692, 737, 787, 806, 808, 812, 813, 817, 862, 888, 900, 902, 930, 939, 960, 964, 975].

240 Etienne, A. "Etude du récit de l'événement de Pentecôte dans Actes 2," *FV* 80/1 (1981): 47-67 [*see also* 001, 043, 076, 077, 078, 088, 101, 110, 121, 126, 154, 178, 190, 221, 239, 242, 300, 340, 370, 465, 493, 512, 528, 541, 577, 590, 611, 613, 624, 644, 665, 687, 692, 737, 787, 806, 808, 812, 813, 817, 862, 888, 900, 902, 930, 939, 960, 964, 975].

241 Eulenstein, Rolf. "Die wundersame Befreiung des Petrus aus Todesgefahr, Acta 12,1-23," *WD* 12 (1973): 43-69.

242 Evans, C. A. "The Prophetic Setting of the Pentecost Sermon," *ZNW* 74/1-2 (1983): 148-50 [*see also* 644].

243 Exum, C. and C. Talbert. "The Structure of Paul's Speech to the Ephesian Elders (Acts 20:18-35)," *CBQ* 29/2 (1967): 233-36 [*see also* 090, 448, 700].

244 Fackre, G. "An Acts Theology of Evangelism," *ReL* 44 (1975): 73-89 [*see also* 407, 802].

245 Fahy, T. "The Council of Jerusalem," *ITQ* 30/3 (1963): 232-61 [*see also* 267, 282, 288, 330, 347, 638, 653, 749, 895].

246 _____. "A Phenomenon of Literary Style in Acts of Apostles," *ITQ* 29/4 (1962): 314-18.

247 Fee, Gordon D. "Tongues—Least of the Gifts: Some Exegetical Observations," *Pn* 2/2 (1980): 3-14 [*see also* 001, 011, 012, 025, 201, 230, 239, 266, 279, 322, 346, 437, 483, 552, 665, 722, 808, 932, 973, 975].

248 Felix, F. M. D. "El cristiano, sacramento de Cristo (Act 1,3-11)," *Cist* 20 (1968): 102.

249 Fenasse, J. M. "Paul recontre le magicien Elymas," *BTS* 136 (1971): 14 [*see also* 008, 146, 981].

250 _____. "Pierre et Corneille, Le Centurion," *BTS* 41 (1961): 4-5 [*see also* 108, 129, 360, 542, 573, 587, 658, 688, 838, 873].

251 Fensham, F. C. "The Convention of Jerusalem: A Turning Point in the History of the Church (Afrikaans)," *NGTT* 10 (1969): 32-38 [*see also* 029, 178, 234, 245, 281, 408, 414, 461, 617, 662, 711, 713, 758, 847, 857].

252 Fenton, John. "The Order of the Miracles Performed by Peter and Paul in Acts," *ET* 72/12 (1966): 381-83 [*see also* 371, 433].

253 Ferguson, Everett. "Apologetics in the NT (Acts)," *RQ* 6 (1962): 189-96.

254 _____. "The Hellenists in the Book of Acts," *RQ* 12/4 (1969): 159-80 [*see also* 397, 526, 703, 710, 728, 736, 958].

255 _____. "Qumran and Codex 'D'," *RQum* 8/29 (1972): 75-80 [*see also* 038, 146, 233, 262, 420, 513, 597, 804, 805, 947].

256 Fernández y Fernández, J. "El manuscrito de Pedro de Valencia que ileva por título en su portada: 'Una gran parte de la Estoria Apostólica en los Actos y en la Epístola ad Gálatas,' " *CuBi* 34 (1977): 155.

257 Fernandez, Pedro. "Los factores historicos: su presencia en las communidades del Nuevo Testamento (Hech. 1-15) y su importancia ecumenica actual," *DE* 15 (1980): 201-25.

258 Ferraro, G. "*Kairoi anapsyxeōs.* Annotazioni su Atti 3,20," *RBib* 23/1 (1975): 67-78 [*see also* 268, 294, 318, 319, 383, 402, 593, 919, 941].

259 Feuillet, A. "Le 'Commencement' de l'économie Chrétienne d'après He ii.304, Mc i.1 et Ac i.1-2," *NTS* 24 (1978): 163-74.

260 Filippini, R. "Atti 3,1-10: Proposta di analisi del racconto," *RBib* 28/3 (1980): 305-17.

261 Filson, F. V. "Live Issues in the Acts," *BiR* 9 (1964): 26-37.

262 Fitzmyer, Joseph A. "David, 'Being Therefore a Prophet . . . ' (Acts 2:30)," *CBQ* 34/3 (1972): 332-39 [*see also* 223].

263 Folliet, G. "Les citations de *Actes* 17,28 et *Tite* 1,12 chez Augustin," *REA* 11/3-4 (1965): 293-95.

264 Fornberg, Tord. "An Early Church in a Pluralistic Society," *CBQ* 41 (1979): 333 [*see also* 031, 056, 191, 228, 229, 238, 302, 316, 455].

265 Foulkes, I. W. "Two Semantic Problems in the Translation of Acts 4:5-20," *BiTr* 29/1 (1978): 121-25.

266 Fowler, J. R. "Holiness, the Spirit's Infilling, and Speaking with Tongues," *Para* 2 (1968): 7-9 [*see also* 001, 011, 012, 025, 201, 230, 239, 247, 279, 322, 346, 437, 483, 552, 665, 722, 808, 932, 973, 975].

267 France, R. T. "Barnabas—Son of Encouragement," *ERT* 4/1 (1980): 91-101 [*see also* 245, 282, 288, 330, 347, 638, 653, 749, 895].

268 Francis, F. O. "Eschatology and History in Luke-Acts," *JAAR* 37 (1969): 49-63 [*see also* 258, 294, 318, 319, 383, 402, 593, 919, 941].

269 Franklin, E. "The Ascension and the Eschatology of Luke-Acts," *SJT* 23/2 (1970): 191-200 [*see also* 055, 154, 175, 207, 210, 274, 335, 368, 369, 462, 506, 508, 531, 536, 539, 540, 612, 614, 793, 827, 959, 977].

270 Fransen, Irenée. "Le baptême de l'eunuque: Philippe baptise un Ethopien," *BTS* 72 (1965): 18-19 [*see also* 152, 196, 315, 324, 448, 488, 603, 673, 699, 817, 907, 974].

271 _____. "Par le nom de Jésus Christ le Nazaréen. Acts 4,8-12," *BibVie* 59 (1964): 38-44.

272 Frantzen, P. "Das 'Zeichen des Jonas,' " *TGl* 57/1 (1967): 61-66.

273 Freire, C. Escudero. " 'Kata Agnoian' (Hch 3,17). ¿Disculpa o acusación?" *Com* 9/2-3 (1976): 221-31.

274 Frey, C. "Die Himmelfahrtsbericht des Lukas nach Apg 1:1-12. Exegetische und didaktische Problematik," *KB* 95 (1970): 10-21 [*see also* 055, 154, 175, 207, 210, 269, 335, 368, 369, 462, 506, 508, 531, 536, 539, 540, 612, 614, 793, 827, 959, 977].

275 Fuchs, Ernst. "Meditationen zu Ernest Haenchens Kommentar Über die lukanische Apostelgeschichte," *VF* 1 (1960): 67-70.

276 Fudge, E. "Paul's Apostolic Self-Consciousness at Athens," *JETS* 14/3 (1971): 193-98 [*see also* 017, 020, 086, 091, 132, 394, 509, 604, 635, 680, 725, 852, 980].

277 Fuente, A. Glz. "El Espiritu Santo y los sacramentos: el dato Biblico," *Ang* 55 (1978): 366-414 [*see also* 006, 042, 064, 076, 078, 084, 100, 126, 128, 148, 189, 195, 196, 309, 312, 315, 319, 320, 322, 327, 371, 372, 387, 403, 439, 459, 462, 475, 482, 519, 522, 528, 532, 541, 549, 574, 586, 590, 609, 611, 614, 623, 632, 643, 692, 699, 709, 737, 755, 759, 772, 783, 784, 808, 817, 830, 864, 867, 872, 891, 894, 898, 900, 913, 917, 919, 934, 939, 944, 960, 964, 974].

278 Fuller, R. J. "The Choice of Matthias," *SEv* 5 (1973): 140-46 [*see also* 038, 187, 425, 537, 654, 787, 963, 970].

279 _____. "Tongues in the New Testament," *ACQ* 3 (1963): 162-68 [*see also* 001, 011, 012, 025, 201, 230, 239, 247, 266, 322, 346, 437, 483, 552, 665, 722, 808, 932, 973, 975].

280 Fusco, V. "Le sezioni-noi degli Atti nella discussione recente," *BibO* 25/2 (1983): 73-86 [*see also* 047, 069, 151, 155, 156, 163, 166, 329, 476, 615, 841, 949, 984].

281 Gaechter, P. "Geschichtliches zum Apostelkonzil," *ZKT* 85/3 (1963): 339-54 [*see also* 029, 178, 234, 245, 251, 408, 414, 461, 617, 662, 711, 713, 758, 847, 857].

282 Gaertner, B. "Paulus und Barnabas in Lystra. Zu Apg. 14.8-15," *SEÅ* 27 (1962): 83-88 [*see also* 245, 267, 288, 330, 347, 638, 653, 749, 895].

283 Galanis, J. L. "Ta idiaitera charaktēristika stē diēgēsē tōn Praxeōn gia tē metabasē kai to ergo tou Paulou stous Philippous se schesē me to prosōpo tou syngraphea," *DBM* 9/2 (1980): 63-76 [*see also* 028 182, 280, 366, 734, 783, 788, 789].

284 Gallazzi, C. "P. Mil. Vogl. Inv. 1224: Novum Testamentum, Act. 2,30-37 e 2,46-3,2," *BASP* 9/1-2 (1982): 39-45.

285 Gamba, G. G. "Significato letterale e portate dottrinale dell'inciso participiale di Atti 2,47b: *echontes charin pros holon ton laon*," *Salm* 43/1 (1981): 45-70.

286 Gangel, Kenneth O. "Paul's Areopagus Speech," *BS* 127/508 (1970): 308-12 [*see also* 091, 098, 132, 197, 231, 394, 509, 518, 577, 635, 725, 728, 730, 852].

287 Garralda J. and J. Casaretto. "Uso del Antiquo Testamento en los primeros capitulos de 'Hechos,' " *RBib* 28/1 (1966): 35-39.

288 Gärtner, B. "Paulus und Barnabas in Lystra. Zu Apg. 14, 8-15," *SEÅ* 27 (1962): 83-88 [*see also* 245, 267, 282, 330, 347, 638, 653, 749, 895].

289 Gasque, W. W. "Did Luke Have Access to Traditions about the Apostles and the Early Churches?" *JETS* 17/1 (1974): 45-48 [*see also* 198, 356, 454, 499].

290 _____. "The Historical Value of the Book of Acts: An Essay in the History of New Testament Cricitism," *EQ* 41/2 (1969): 68-88.

291 _____. "A History of the Criticism of the Acts," *TL* 104 (1979): 193-96.

292 _____. "La valeur historique des Actes des Apôtres," *Hok* 3 (1976): 82-92.

293 _____. "La valeur historique des Actes des Apôtres (2d partie)," *Hok* 6 (1977): 12-33.

294 Gaventa, B. R. "The Eschatology of Luke-Acts Revisited," *En* 43/1 (1982): 27-42 [*see also* 258, 268, 318, 319, 383, 402, 593, 919, 941].

295 _____. " 'You Will Be My Witnesses': Aspects of Mission in the Acts of the Apostles," *Miss* 10/4 (1982): 413-25 [*see also* 136, 149, 200, 359, 518, 522, 538, 558, 591, 646, 683, 703, 848, 905, 961].

296 Gerhardsson, Birger. "Einige Bemerkungen zu Apg 4,32," *ST* 24/2 (1970): 142-49 [*see also* 003, 021, 133, 308, 355, 445, 512, 551, 569, 632, 703, 777, 801, 810, 897, 927, 928].

297 _____. "Några anmärkningar till Apg 4:32," *SEÅ* 35 (1970): 96-103.

298 Gewalt, D. "Neutestamentliche Exegese und Soziologie," *EvT* 31 (1971): 87-99.

299 Ghidelli, C. "Atti degli Apostoli (Testo greco, apparato critico, passi parallile, versione ital, commento)," *Stud* 75 (1979): 420.

300 _____. "Gli Atti degli Apostoli nella Chiesa oggi. Bollettino Bliografico," *RCI* 53 (1972): 220-27 [*see also* 001, 043, 076, 077, 078, 088, 101, 110, 121, 126, 154, 178, 190, 221, 239, 240, 242, 340, 370, 465, 493, 512, 528, 541, 577, 590, 611, 613, 624, 644, 665, 687, 692, 737, 787, 806, 808, 812, 813, 817, 862, 888, 900, 902, 930, 939, 960, 964, 975].

301 _____. "Un saggio di lettura dell'AT nel libro degli Atti (Atti 13,33-35)," *PV* 9 (1964): 83-91.

302 _____. "Situazioni di peccato secondo il libro degli Atti," *ScuC* 106/3-4 (1978): 253-65 [*see also* 031, 056, 191, 228, 229, 238, 264, 316, 455].

303 _____. "Studi sugli Atti degli Apostoli," *ScuC* 93/Supp 3 (1965): 390-98 [*see also* 067, 082, 304, 341, 357, 409, 576].

304 _____. "Tre recenti commenti in lingua tedesca agli Atti degli Apostoli," *ScuC* 93/Supp 3 (1965): 371-89 [*see also* 067, 082, 303, 341, 357, 409, 576].

305 Gibbs, J. M. "Canon Cuming's Service-Endings in the Epistles: A Rejoinder," *NTS* 24 (1978): 545-47.

306 _____. ''Luke 24:13-33 and Acts 8:26-39. The Emmaus Incident and Eunuch's Baptism as Parallel Stories,'' *NRT* 103 (1981): 360-74 [*see also* 134, 343, 625].

307 Gibert, P. ''L'invention d'un genre littéraire,'' *LV* 30/153-54 (1981): 19-33.

308 _____. ''Les premiers chrétiens d'après les Actes des Apôtres,'' *Chr* 18/70 (1971): 219-28 [*see also* 003, 021, 133, 296, 355, 445, 512, 551, 569, 632, 703, 777, 801, 810, 897, 927, 928].

309 Giblet, J. ''Baptism in the Spirit in the Acts of the Apostles,'' *OC* 10 (1974): 162-71 [*see also* 006, 042, 064, 076, 078, 084, 100, 126, 128, 148, 189, 195, 196, 204, 205, 277, 309, 312, 315, 319, 320, 322, 327, 371, 372, 387, 403, 439, 459, 462, 475, 482, 519, 522, 528, 532, 541, 549, 574, 586, 590, 609, 611, 614, 623, 632, 643, 692, 699, 709, 737, 755, 759, 772, 783, 784, 808, 817, 830, 864, 867, 872, 891, 894, 898, 900, 913, 917, 919, 934, 939, 944, 960, 964, 974].

310 Giblin, C. H. ''Complementarity of Symbolic Event and Discourse in Acts 2,1-40,'' *TU* 112 (1973): 189-96.

311 _____. ''A Prophetic Vision of History and Things (Acts 6:8-8:3),'' *BibTo* 63 (1972): 994:1001.

312 Geisen, H. ''Der Heilige Geist als Ursprung und treibende Kraft des christlichen Lebens. Zu den Geistaussagen der Apostelgeschichte,'' *BiKi* 37/4 (1982): 126-32 [*see also* 006, 042, 064, 076, 078, 084, 100, 126, 128, 148, 189, 195, 196, 277, 309, 315, 319, 320, 322, 327, 371, 372, 387, 403, 439, 459, 462, 475, 482, 519, 522, 528, 532, 541, 549, 574, 586, 590, 609, 611, 614, 623, 632, 643, 692, 699, 709, 737, 755, 759, 772, 783, 784, 808, 817, 830, 864, 867, 872, 891, 894, 898, 900, 913, 917, 919, 934, 939, 944, 960, 964, 974].

313 Giet, Stanislaus. ''Exégèse,'' *RScR* 41 (1967): 341-48.

314 Gilchrist, J. M. ''On What Charge Was St. Paul Brought to Rome?'' *ET* 78/9 (1967): 264-66 [*see also* 637, 782, 820, 912].

315 Giles, K. "Is Luke an Exponent of 'Early Protestantism'? Church Order in the Lukan Writings (Part 1)," *EQ* 54/4 (1982): 193-205 [*see also* 152, 196, 270, 324, 448, 488, 603, 673, 699, 817, 907, 974].

316 _____. "Is Luke an Exponent of 'Early Protestantism'? Church Order in the Lukan Writings (continued)," *EQ* 55/1 (1983): 3-20 [*see also* 031, 056, 191, 228, 229, 238, 264, 302, 455].

317 Giles, K. "Luke's Use of the Term ekklēsia with Special Reference to Acts 20:28 and 9:31," *NTS* 31/1 (1985): 135-42.

318 _____. "Present-Future Eschatology in the Book of Acts (I)," *RefTR* 40/3 (1981): 65-71 [*see also* 258, 268, 294, 319, 383, 402, 593, 919, 941].

319 _____. "Present-Future Eschatology in the Book of Acts (II)," *RefTR* 41/1 (1982): 11-18 [*see also* 006, 042, 064, 076, 078, 084, 100, 126, 128, 148, 189, 195, 196, 277, 309, 312, 315, 320, 322, 327, 371, 372, 387, 403, 439, 459, 462, 475, 482, 519, 522, 528, 532, 541, 549, 574, 586, 590, 609, 611, 614, 623, 632, 643, 692, 699, 709, 737, 755, 759, 772, 783, 784, 808, 817, 830, 864, 867, 872, 891, 894, 898, 900, 913, 917, 919, 934, 939, 944, 960, 964, 974].

320 _____. "Salvation in Lukan Theology: Salvation in the Book of Acts," *RefTR* 42/2 (1983): 45-49 [*see also* 006, 042, 064, 076, 078, 084, 100, 126, 128, 148, 189, 195, 196, 277, 309, 312, 315, 319, 322, 327, 371, 372, 387, 403, 439, 459, 462, 475, 482, 519, 522, 528, 532, 541, 549, 574, 586, 590, 609, 611, 614, 623, 632, 643, 692, 699, 709, 737, 755, 759, 772, 783, 784, 808, 817, 830, 864, 867, 872, 891, 894, 898, 900, 913, 917, 919, 934, 939, 944, 960, 964, 974].

321 Gill, D. "The Structure of Acts 9," *Bib* 55/4 (1974): 546-48.

322 Gilmour, S. MacLean. "Easter and Pentecost," *JBL* 81/1 (1962): 62-66 [*see also* 006, 042, 064, 076, 078, 084, 100, 126, 128, 148, 189, 195, 196, 277, 309, 312, 315, 319, 320, 327, 371, 372, 387, 403, 439, 459, 462, 475, 482, 519, 522, 528, 532, 541, 549, 574, 586, 590, 609, 611, 614, 623, 632, 643, 692, 699, 709, 737, 755, 759, 772, 783, 784, 808, 817, 830, 864, 867, 872, 891, 894, 898, 900, 913, 917, 919, 934, 939, 944, 960, 964, 974].

323 Girlanda, A. "De Conversione Pauli in Actibus Apostolorum
tripliciter narrata," *VD* 39/2 (1961): 66-81; 39/3 (1961): 129-
40; 39/4 (1961): 173-84 [*see also* 035, 100, 148, 167, 178,
232, 372, 503, 504, 564, 609, 661, 739, 760, 777, 784, 812,
850, 854, 869, 870, 890, 895, 941, 971, 984, 987].

324 Glaser, Gerhard. "Das biblische Pfingsten und unser Pfingsten," *GeL* 52/3 (1979): 164-70 [*see also* 152, 196, 270, 315,
448, 488, 603, 673, 699, 817, 907, 974].

325 Glasson, T. Francis. "St. Paul, Virgil and the Sibyl," *LQHR* 37/
1 (1968): 70-76.

326 _____. "The Speeches in Acts and Thucydides," *ET* 76/5
(1965): 165 [*see also* 070, 096, 115, 193, 199, 497, 554, 647,
839, 846, 867, 921, 968].

327 Glombitza, O. "Zur Charakterisierung des Stephanus in Act 6
und 7," *ZNW* 53/3-4 (1962): 238-44 [*see also* 006, 042, 064,
076, 078, 084, 100, 126, 128, 148, 189, 195, 196, 277, 309,
312, 315, 319, 320, 322, 371, 372, 387, 403, 439, 459, 462,
475, 482, 519, 522, 528, 532, 541, 549, 574, 586, 590, 609,
611, 614, 623, 632, 643, 692, 699, 709, 737, 755, 759, 772,
783, 784, 808, 817, 830, 864, 867, 872, 891, 894, 898, 900,
913, 917, 919, 934, 939, 944, 960, 964, 974].

328 _____. "Der Schluss der Petrusrede Acta 2:36-40. Ein Beitrag zum Problem der Predigten in Acta," *ZNW* 52/1-2
(1961): 115-18 [*see also* 050, 107, 162, 176, 181, 219, 245,
250, 252, 414, 498, 640, 645, 658, 672, 711, 785, 787, 815,
942, 964, 965].

329 _____. "Der Schritt nach Europa: Erwägungen zu Apg 16,9-
15," *ZNW* 53/1-2 (1962): 77-82 [*see also* 047, 069, 151, 155,
156, 163, 166, 280, 476, 615, 841, 949, 984].

330 Glover, R. " 'Luke and the Antiochene' and Acts," *NTS* 11/1
(1964): 97-106 [*see also* 245, 267, 282, 288, 347, 638, 653,
749, 895].

331 Glynne, W. "Psychology and the Book of Acts," *ChQR* 106
(1928): 281-300.

332 Godin, A. "Histoire d'un deuil et d'un souffle nouveau," *LV* 30/ 153-54 (1981): 123-39 [*see also* 173, 176, 336, 559, 567, 654, 687, 763].

333 Goff, W. "La etica activa en el libro de los Hechos," *D* 5 (1975): 28-32.

334 Goldsmith, Dale. "Acts 13:33-37: A *Pesher* on 2 Samuel 7," *JBL* 87/3 (1968): 321-24 [*see also* 024, 055, 058, 077, 142, 168, 223, 343, 363, 386, 458, 462, 506, 508, 609, 675, 678, 683, 756, 763, 803, 832, 862, 950].

335 Gooding, D. W. "Demythologizing Old and New, and Luke's Description of the Ascension: A Layman's Appraisal," *IBS* 2 (1980): 95-119 [*see also* 055, 154, 175, 207, 210, 269, 274, 368, 369, 462, 506, 508, 531, 536, 539, 540, 612, 614, 793, 827, 959, 977].

336 Gordon, A. B. "The Fate of Judas According to Acts 1:18," *EQ* 44/2 (1971): 97-100 [*see also* 173, 176, 332, 559, 567, 654, 687, 763].

337 Gordon, R. P. "Targumic Parallels to Acts XIII 18 and Didache XIV 3," *NT* 16/4 (1974): 285-89.

338 Gorg, Manfred. "Apg 2,9-11 in außerbiblischer Sicht," *BN* 1 (1976): 15-18.

339 Gourgues, M. "Exalté à la droite de Dieu (Ac 2,33; 5,31)," *SE* 27 (1975): 303-27 [*see also* 952].

340 _____. "Lecture christologique du Psaume CX et fête de la Pentecôte," *RB* 83 (1976): 5-24 [*see also* 001, 043, 076, 077, 078, 088, 101, 110, 121, 126, 154, 178, 190, 221, 239, 240, 242, 300, 370, 465, 493, 512, 528, 541, 577, 590, 611, 613, 624, 644, 665, 687, 692, 737, 787, 806, 808, 812, 813, 817, 862, 888, 900, 902, 930, 939, 960, 964, 975].

341 Grässer, E. "Acta-Forschung seit 1960," *TRu* 41/2 (1976): 141- 94; 41/3 (1976): 259-90; 42/1 (1977): 1-68 [*see also* 067, 082, 303, 304, 357, 409, 576].

342 _____. "Die Apostelgeschichte in der Forschung der Gegenwart," *TR* 26/2 (1960): 93-167 [*see also* 120, 342, 453, 518, 619, 852, 952].

343 Grassi, J. S. "Emmaus Revisited (Luke 24:13-35 and Acts 8:26-40)" *CBQ* 26/4 (1964): 463-67 [*see also* 134, 306, 625].

344 Green, E. M. B. "Syria and Cilicia: A Note," *ET* 71/2 (1959): 52-53.

345 Green, W. M. "Apostels—Actes 14:14," *RQ* 4 (1960): 245-47 [*see also* 212, 220, 723].

346 _____. "Glossolalia in the Second Century," *RQ* 16 (1973): 99-126 [*see also* 001, 011, 012, 025, 201, 230, 239, 247, 266, 279, 322, 437, 483, 552, 665, 722, 808, 932, 973, 975].

347 Grelot, P. "Note sur Actes, XIII, 47," *RB* 88/3 (1981): 368-72 [*see also* 245, 267, 282, 288, 330, 638, 653, 749, 895].

348 Griffiths, J. G. "Was Damaris an Egyptian? (Acts 17:34)," *BZ* 8/2 (1964): 293-95.

349 Grimalt, Sureda M. "Los Hechos de los Apóstoles, su estructura y fisonomia," *EF* 72 (1971): 5-17.

350 Grundmann, W. "Der Pfingstbericht der Apostelgeschichte seinem theologischen Sinn," *SEv* 11 (1963): 583-94.

351 Gryglewicz, Feliks. "(Ecclesia Johannea et theologia) Quarti Evangeli," *RBL* 32 (1979): 34-46.

352 Grzybek, S. "Wprowadzenie w Dzieje Apostolskie (Dz 1,1-2)," *RBL* 19/1 (1966): 51-56.

353 Guillet, J. "Die Bezeugung der Auferstehung nach der Apostelgeschichte," *IKZ* 11/1 (1982): 21-31.

354 _____. "L'ingresso alla chiesa secondo gli Atti Apostoli," *SIC* 5/27 (1976): 10-21.

355 Guillet, P. E. T. "Réflexions sur les origines du christianisme. Bordeau 1977," *CahC* 26 (1978): 101-104 [*see also* 003, 021, 133, 296, 308, 445, 512, 551, 569, 632, 703, 777, 801, 810, 897, 927, 928].

356 Gunther, J. J. "The Fate of the Jerusalem Church," *TZ* 29 (1973): 81-94 [*see also* 198, 289, 454, 499].

357 Guthrie, D. "Recent Literature on the Acts of the Apostles," *VE* 2 (1963): 33-49 [*see also* 067, 082, 303, 304, 341, 409, 576].

358 Güting, E. "Der geographische Horizont der sogenannten Völkerliste des Lukas (Acta 2,9-11)," *ZNW* 66/3-4 (1975): 149-69 [*see also* 053, 245, 427, 429, 430, 545].

359 Guy, Cal. "The Missionary Message of Acts," *SWJT* 17/1 (1974): 49-64 [*see also* 136, 149, 200, 295, 518, 522, 538, 558, 591, 646, 683, 703, 848, 905, 961].

360 Haacker, K. "Dibelius und Cornelius. Ein Beispiel formgeschichtlicher Überlieferungskritik," *BZ* 24/2 (1980): 234-51 [*see also* 108, 129, 250, 542, 573, 587, 658, 688, 838, 873].

361 _____. "Die Gallio-Episode und die paulinische Chronologie," *BZ* 16/2 (1972): 252-55 [*see also* 731].

362 Haenchen, E. "Die Apostelgeschichte," *EQ* 50 (1977): 121.

363 _____. "Judentum und Christentum in der Apostelgeschichte," *ZNW* 54/3-4 (1963): 155-87 [*see also* 144, 382, 427, 449, 524, 538, 683, 701, 774, 782, 935, 944, 969].

364 _____. "Quellenanalyse und Kompositionsanalyse in Apg 15," *BZNW* 26 (1960): 153-64 [*see also* 093, 765].

365 _____. "Simon Magus in der Apostelgeschichte," *GNT* (1973): 267-79 [*see also* 008, 037, 048, 174, 670, 799, 868].

366 _____. " 'We' in Acts and the Itinerary," *JTC* 1 (1965): 65-99 [*see also* 028 182, 280, 283, 734, 783, 788, 789].

367 Haenchen, E. and P. Weigandt. "The Original Text of Acts?" *NTS* 14/4 (1968): 469-81 [*see also* 060, 237, 358, 377, 378, 460, 490, 511, 537, 578, 698, 789, 827, 862, 896, 908, 910, 914, 926, 955, 970, 977].

368 Hagemeyer, O. "Ihr seid meine Zeugen," *EA* 42/5 (1966): 375-84 [*see also* 055, 154, 175, 207, 210, 269, 274, 335, 369, 462, 506, 508, 531, 536, 539, 540, 612, 614, 793, 827, 959, 977].

369 Hahn, F. "Die Himmelfahrt Jesu. Ein Gespräch Lohfink," *Bib* 55 (1974): 418-26 [*see also* 055, 154, 175, 207, 210, 269, 274, 335, 368, 462, 506, 508, 531, 536, 539, 540, 612, 614, 793, 827, 959, 977].

370 van Halsema, J. H. "De historischen betrouwbaarheid van het Pinksterverhaal," *NTT* 20/2 (1966): 218 [*see also* 001, 043, 076, 077, 078, 088, 101, 110, 121, 126, 154, 178, 190, 221, 239, 240, 242, 300, 340, 465, 493, 512, 528, 541, 577, 590, 611, 613, 624, 644, 665, 687, 692, 737, 787, 806, 808, 812, 813, 817, 862, 888, 900, 902, 930, 939, 960, 964, 975].

371 Hamblin, R. L. "Miracles in the Book of Acts," *SWJT* 17/1 (1974): 19-34 [*see also* 006, 042, 064, 076, 078, 084, 100, 126, 128, 148, 189, 195, 196, 277, 309, 312, 315, 319, 320, 322, 327, 372, 387, 403, 439, 459, 462, 475, 482, 519, 522, 528, 532, 541, 549, 574, 586, 590, 609, 611, 614, 623, 632, 643, 692, 699, 709, 737, 755, 759, 772, 783, 784, 808, 817, 830, 864, 867, 872, 891, 894, 898, 900, 913, 917, 919, 934, 939, 944, 960, 964, 974].

372 Hamel, E. "La legge nouva per una comunità nuova," *CC* 124(1973): 351-60 [*see also* 006, 042, 064, 076, 078, 084, 100, 126, 128, 148, 189, 195, 196, 277, 309, 312, 315, 319, 320, 322, 327, 371, 387, 403, 439, 459, 462, 475, 482, 519, 522, 528, 532, 541, 549, 574, 586, 590, 609, 611, 614, 623, 632, 643, 692, 699, 709, 737, 755, 759, 772, 783, 784, 808, 817, 830, 864, 867, 872, 891, 894, 898, 900, 913, 917, 919, 934, 939, 944, 960, 964, 974].

373 Hamm, D. "Acts 3:12-26: Peter's Speech and the Healing of the Man Born Lame," *PRS* 11/3 (1984): 199-217.

374 Hanford, W. R. "Deutero-Isaiah and Luke-Acts: Straightforward Universalism?" *ChQR* 168/367 (1967): 141-52 [*see also* 010, 016, 423, 466, 482, 488, 502, 533, 555, 581, 626, 629, 677, 792, 863, 900, 953].

375 Hansack, E. "Er lebte . . . von seinem eigenen Einkommen (Apg 28,30)," *BZ* 19/2 (1975): 249-53.

376 _____. "Nochmals zu Apostelgeschichte 28,30. Erwiderung auf F. Saums kritische Anmerkungen," *BZ* 21/1 (1977): 118-21.

377 Hanson, R. P. C. "The Ideology of Codex Bezae in Acts," *NTS* 14 (1967-1968): 282-86 [*see also* 160, 162, 166, 553, 695, 714, 909].

378 _____. ''The Provenance of the Interpolator in the 'Western' Text of Acts and of Acts Itself,'' *NTS* 12/3 (1965-1966): 211-30 [*see also* 060, 237, 358, 367, 377, 460, 490, 511, 537, 578, 698, 789, 827, 862, 896, 908, 910, 914, 926, 955, 970, 977].

379 Harlé, Paul. ''Un 'Private-Joke' de Paul dans le livre des Actes (XXVI.28-29),'' *NTS* 24/4 (1978): 527-33.

380 Harrison, E. F. ''Acts: The Expanding Church 1975,'' *AsbS* 33/3 (1978): 43.

381 Hartman, L. ''Davids son. Apropå Acta 13,16-41,'' *SEÅ* 28-29 (1963-1964): 117-34.

382 Hasler, V. ''Judenmission und Judenschuld,'' *TZ* 24 (1968): 173-90 [*see also* 144, 363, 427, 449, 524, 538, 683, 701, 774, 782, 935, 944, 969].

383 Haubst, R. ''Eschatologie, 'Der Wetterwinkel'—'Theologie der Hoffnung,' '' *TTZ* 77 (1968): 365 [*see also* 258, 268, 294, 318, 319, 402, 593, 919, 941].

384 Haulotte, Edgar. ''Actes des Apôtres. Un guide de lecture,'' *ETR* 54 (1979): 170.

385 _____. ''Fondation d'une communauté de type universel: Actes 10,1-11,18. Étude critique sur la rédaction, la 'structure' et la 'tradition' du récit,'' *RSR* 58/1 (1970): 63-100 [*see also* 201, 398, 420].

386 _____. ''La vie en communion, phase ultime de al Pentecôte, Actes 2,42-47,'' *FV* 80/1 (1981): 69-75 [*see also* 024, 055, 058, 077, 142, 168, 223, 334, 343, 363, 458, 462, 506, 508, 609, 675, 678, 683, 756, 763, 803, 832, 862, 950].

387 Haya-Prats, G. ''L'Esprit force de l'Eglise . . . Acts,'' *RBib* 26 (1978): 434-37 [*see also* 006, 042, 064, 076, 078, 084, 100, 126, 128, 148, 189, 195, 196, 277, 309, 312, 315, 319, 320, 322, 327, 371, 372, 403, 439, 459, 462, 475, 482, 519, 522, 528, 532, 541, 549, 574, 586, 590, 609, 611, 614, 623, 632, 643, 692, 699, 709, 737, 755, 759, 772, 783, 784, 808, 817, 830, 864, 867, 872, 891, 894, 898, 900, 913, 917, 919, 934, 939, 944, 960, 964, 974].

388 Hazelton, J. S. "El problema de la revelación en el Libro de los Hechos," *CuT* 2 (1972): 213-29.

389 Hedrick, C. W. "Paul's Conversion/Call: A Comparative Analysis of the Three Reports in Acts," *JBL* 100/3 (1981): 415-32 [*see also* 457, 516, 607, 804, 882].

390 Heinzel, E. "Zum Kult der Artemis en Ephesos," *JOAI* 50 (1972): 243-51 [*see also* 088, 436, 451, 467, 674, 700, 868, 924].

391 Hemer, C. J. "The Adjective 'Phrygia,' " *JTS* 27/1 (1976): 122-26 [*see also* 395].

392 _____. "Euraquilo and Melita," *JTS* 26/1 (1975): 100-11 [*see also* 001, 605].

393 _____. "Luke the Historian," *BJRL* 60/1 (1977): 28-51.

394 _____. "Paul at Athens: A Topographical Note," *NTS* 20/3 (1974): 341-50 [*see also* 017, 020, 086, 091, 132, 276, 509, 604, 635, 680, 725, 852, 980].

395 _____. "Phrygia: A Further Note," *JTS* 28/1 (1977): 99-101 [*see also* 395].

396 Hengel, M. "Der Historiker Lukas und die Geographie Palästinas in der Apostelgeschichte," *ZDP* 99 (1983): 147-83.

397 _____. "Zwischen Jesus und Paulus. Die 'Hellenisten,' die 'Sieben' und Stephanus (Apg 6,1-15; 7,54-8,3)," *ZTK* 72/2 (1975): 151-206 [*see also* 254, 526, 703, 728, 736, 958].

398 Herman, I. Z. "Un tentativo di analisi strutturale di *Atti* 2,41-4,35 secundo il metodo di A. J. Greimas," *Anton* 56/2-3 (1981): 467-74 [*see also* 385].

399 Herrmann, T. "Die Bruderliebe nach dem hl. Johannes im Lichte der Synoptiker und des hl. Paulus," *STV* 17 (1979): 43-64.

400 Heutger, N. " 'Paulus auf Malta' im Lichte der maltesischen Topographie," *BZ* 28/1 (1984): 86-88.

401 Hezel, F. X. " 'Conversion' and 'Repentance' in Lucan Theology," *BibTo* 37 (1968): 2596-2602 [*see also* 206, 213, 457, 563, 621, 670, 691, 873, 874, 906].

402 Hiers, R. H. "The Problems of the Delay of the Parousia in Luke-Acts," *NTS* 20 (1974): 145-55 [*see also* 258, 268, 294, 318, 319, 383, 593, 919, 941].

403 Hill, D. "The Spirit and the Church's Witness: Observations on Acts 1:6-8," *IBS* 6/1 (1984): 16-26 [*see also* 006, 042, 064, 076, 078, 084, 100, 126, 128, 148, 189, 195, 196, 277, 309, 312, 315, 319, 320, 322, 327, 371, 372, 387, 439, 459, 462, 475, 482, 519, 522, 528, 532, 541, 549, 574, 586, 590, 609, 611, 614, 623, 632, 643, 692, 699, 709, 737, 755, 759, 772, 783, 784, 808, 817, 830, 864, 867, 872, 891, 894, 898, 900, 913, 917, 919, 934, 939, 944, 960, 964, 974].

404 Hock, Ronald F. "Paul's Tentmaking and the Problem of his Social Class," *JBL* 97 (1978): 555-64.

405 _____. "The Workshop as a Social Setting for Paul's Missionary Preaching," *CBQ* 41/3 (1979): 438-50 [*see also* 794].

406 Hoerber, R. G. "The Decree of Claudius in Acts 18:2," *CTM* 31 (1960): 690-94.

407 _____. "Evangelism in Acts," *CJ* 7/3 (1981): 89-90 [*see also* 244, 802].

408 _____. "A Review of the Apostolic Council After 1925 Years," *CJ* 2/4 (1976): 155-59 [*see also* 029, 178, 234, 245, 251, 281, 414, 461, 617, 662, 711, 713, 758, 847, 857].

409 _____. "Several Classics Reprinted: On the Language of the New Testament and the Reliability of Acts," *CJ* 5/2 (1979): 63-65 [*see also* 067, 082, 303, 304, 341, 357, 576].

410 Holtz, T. "Die Bedeutung des Apostelkonzils für Paulus," *NT* 1 (1974): 110-33.

411 Hordern, Rick. "Paul as a Theological Authority," *USQR* 33/3-4 (1978): 133-49.

412 van der Horst, P. W. "Drohung und Hord schnaubend (Acta 9,1)," *NT* 12/3 (1970): 257-69.

413 _____. "Hellenistic Parallels to the Acts of the Apostles: 1:1-26," *ZNW* 74/1-2 (1983): 17-26.

414 _____. "Peter's Shadow: The Religio-Historical Background of Acts 5:15," *NTS* 23/2 (1977): 204-12 [*see also* 029, 178, 234, 245, 251, 281, 408, 461, 617, 662, 711, 713, 758, 847, 857].

415 House, C. "Defilement by Association: Some Insights from the Usage of *koinós/koinóō* in Acts 10 and 11," *AUSS* 21/2 (1983): 143-53 [*see also* 360].

416 Hoyt, H. A. "The Frantic Future and the Christian Directive: Acts 1:8," *GTJ* 10/1 (1969): 36-41.

417 Hubbard, Benjamin J. "Commissioning Stories in Luke-Acts: A Study of Their Antecedents, Form and Content," *Sem* 8 (1977): 103-26.

418 _____. "The Role of Commissioning Accounts in Acts," *PRS* 5 (1978): 187-98.

419 Hug, Joseph. "La prière dans le livre des Actes des Apôtres," *BCPE* 30/5-6 (1978): 38-39.

420 Huuhtanen, Pauli. "Uskovat ja omaisuus Qumranin teksteissä ja Apt:n alkuluvuissa," *TA* 75/4 (1970): 239-54 [*see also* 201, 385].

421 Hyldahl, Niels. "Acta-forskningen—linier og tendenserm" *DTT* 35/1 (1972): 63-70 [*see also* 422].

422 _____. "Die Erforschung der Apostelgeschichte: Linien und Tendenzen," *SNTU* 3 (1978): 159-67.

423 Jacobs, T. "De christologie van de redevoeringen der Handelingen," *Bij* 28/2 (1967): 177-96 [*see also* 010, 016, 374, 466, 482, 488, 502, 533, 555, 581, 626, 629, 677, 792, 863, 900, 953].

424 Jankowski, Gerhard. "Was sollen wir tun? Erwägungen über Apostelgeschichte 2,1-40," *TK* 8 (1980): 22-44.

425 Jaubert, Annie. "L'election de Mattheas et le tirage au sort," *TU* 112 (1973): 267-80 [*see also* 038, 187, 278, 537, 654, 787, 963, 970].

426 Jasper, G. "Der Rat des Jakobus: Das Ringen des Paulus, der Urgemeinde, die Möglichkeit der Mission unter Israel zu erhalten, Apg Kap 21-28," *Jud* 19/3 (1963): 147-62.

427 Jervell, Jacob. "The Acts of the Apostles and the History of Early Christianity," *ST* 37/1 (1983): 17-32 [*see also* 053, 245, 358, 429, 430, 545].

428 _____. "Da fremtiden begynte, Om urkristendommens tro tenkning," *TsTK* 49 (1978): 226.

429 _____. "Das gespaltene Israel und die Heidenvölker. Zur Motivierung der Heidenmission in der Apostelgeschichte," *ST* 19/1-2 (1965): 68-96 [*see also* 053, 245, 358, 427, 430, 545].

430 _____. "Det splittede Israel og folkeslagene. Til motiveringen av hedningemisjonen i apostlenes gjerninger," *NTTid* 66/4 (1965): 232-59 [*see also* 053, 245, 358, 427, 429, 545].

431 _____. "Midt i Israels historie," *NTTid* 69/3 (1968): 130-38 [*see also* 086, 091, 098, 217, 218, 243, 432, 554, 678, 725, 852].

432 _____. "Paulus: der Lehrer Israels. Zu den apologetischen Paulusreden in der Apostelgeschichte," *NT* 10/2-3 (1968): 164-90 [*see also* 086, 091, 098, 217, 218, 243, 431, 554, 678, 725, 852].

433 _____. "Die Zeichen des Apostels. Die Wunder beim lukanischen und paulinischen Paulus," *SNTU* 4 (1979): 54-75 [*see also* 252, 371].

434 _____. "Zur Frage der Traditionsgrundlage der Apostelgeschichte," *ST* 16/1 (1963): 25-41.

435 Johnson, S. E. "Antioch, the Base of Operations," *LTQ* 18/2 (1983): 64-73 [*see also* 106, 129, 184, 201, 454, 498, 527, 554, 601, 701, 895].

436 _____. "The Apostle Paul and the Riot in Ephesus," *LTQ* 15/1 (1979): 79-88 [*see also* 088, 390, 451, 467, 674, 700, 868, 924].

437 Johnson, S. Lewis, Jr. "The Gift of Tongues and the Book of Acts," *BS* 480 (1963): 309-411 [*see also* 001, 011, 012, 025, 201, 230, 239, 247, 266, 279, 322, 346, 483, 552, 665, 722, 808, 932, 973, 975].

438 Jones, P. "Y a-t-il deux types de prophéties dans le Nouveau Testament?" *RevR* 31 (1980): 303-17 [*see also* 973].

439 Journet, C. "La mission visible de l'Esprit-Saint," *RThom* 65
(1965): 357-97 [*see also* 006, 042, 064, 076, 078, 084, 100,
126, 128, 148, 189, 195, 196, 277, 309, 312, 315, 319, 320,
322, 327, 371, 372, 387, 403, 459, 462, 475, 482, 519, 522,
528, 532, 541, 549, 574, 586, 590, 609, 611, 614, 623, 632,
643, 692, 699, 709, 737, 755, 759, 772, 783, 784, 808, 817,
830, 864, 867, 872, 891, 894, 898, 900, 913, 917, 919, 934,
939, 944, 960, 964, 974].

440 Jovino, P. "L'Église communauté des saints dans les 'Actes des
Apôtres' et dans les 'Épitres aux Thessaloniciens,' " *RBib*
16/5 (1968): 495-526 [*see also* 466, 468].

441 Joyce, E. "James, the Just," *BibTo* 1/4 (1963): 256-64.

442 Jozwiak, F. "Meka Chrystusa w Dziejach Apostolskich (Die
Passion Christi in der Apg)," *AKap* 97/3 (1981): 437, 443-
456.

443 _____. "Zycie duchowe pierwotnej wspolnoty chrzescijan-
skiej," *AKap* 84/3 (1975): 424-38.

444 Judge, E. A. "The Decrees of Caesar at Thessalonica," *RefTR*
30/1 (1971): 1-7 [*see also* 163].

445 _____. "Die Frühen Christen als scholastische Gemein-
schaft," *JRH* 1 (1960s): 4-15 [*see also* 003, 021, 133, 296,
308, 355, 512, 551, 569, 632, 703, 777, 801, 810, 897, 927,
928].

446 Judge, E. A. and G. S. R. Thomas. "The Origin of the Church
at Rome: A New Solution (Acts; Rom; Hebr 10:25)," *RefTR*
25 (1966): 81-94.

447 Juel, D. "Social Dimensions of Exegesis: The Use of Psalm 16
in Acts 2," *CBQ* 43/4 (1981): 543-56.

448 Kaiser, Christopher B. "The 'Rebaptism' of the Ephesian
Twelve: Exegetical Study on Acts 19:1-7," *RefTR* 31/1
(1977): 57-61 [*see also* 152, 196, 270, 315, 324, 488, 603,
673, 699, 817, 907, 974].

449 Kaiser, W. C., Jr. "The Davidic Promise and the Inclusion of the Gentiles (Amos 9:9-15 and Acts 15:13-18): A Test Passage for Theological Systems," *JETS* 20/2 (1977): 97-111 [*see also* 144, 363, 382, 427, 524, 538, 683, 701, 774, 782, 935, 944, 969].

450 ——————. "The Promise to David in Psalm 16 and its Application in Acts 2:25-33 and 13:32-37," *JETS* 23 (1980): 219-29.

451 Käsemann, Ernest. "The Disciples of John the Baptist in Ephesus," *BTh* 41 (1964): 136-48 [*see also* 088, 390, 436, 467, 674, 700, 868, 924].

452 ——————. "L'enigma del quarto Vangelo. Giovanni: una communita in conflitto conn il cattolicesimo nascente?" *SacD* 24 (1979): 154.

453 Kasper, W. "Christi Himmelfahrt—Geschichte und theologische Bedeutung," *IKZ* 12/3 (1983): 205-13 [*see also* 120, 342, 518, 619, 852, 952].

454 Kaye, B. N. "Acts' Portrait of Silas," *NTS* 21/1 (1979): 13-26 [*see also* 106, 129, 184, 201, 435, 498, 527, 554, 601, 701, 895].

455 Keck, L. E. "Das Ethos der frühen Christen," *JAAR* 42 (1974): 435-52 [*see also* 031, 056, 191, 228, 229, 238, 264, 302, 316].

456 ——————. "Listening To and Listening For: From Text to Sermon (Acts 1:8)," *Int* 27/2 (1973): 184-202.

457 Kelly, J. "The Conversion of St. Paul," *Emm* 88/10 (1982): 563-65, 576 [*see also* 206, 213, 401, 563, 621, 670, 691, 873, 874, 906].

458 Kepple, R. J. "The Hope of Israel, the Resurrection of the Dead, and Jesus: A Study of Their Relationship in Acts with Particular Regard to the Understanding of Paul's Trial Defense," *JETS* 20/3 (1977): 231-41 [*see also* 024, 055, 058, 077, 142, 168, 223, 334, 343, 363, 386, 462, 506, 508, 609, 675, 677, 678, 683, 756, 763, 803, 832, 862, 950].

459 Kern, W. "Das Fortgehen Jesu und das Kommen des Geistes oder Christi Himmelfahrt," *GeL* 41/2 (1968): 85-90 [*see also* 006, 042, 064, 076, 078, 084, 100, 126, 128, 148, 189, 195, 196, 277, 309, 312, 315, 319, 320, 322, 327, 371, 372, 387, 403, 439, 462, 475, 482, 519, 522, 528, 532, 541, 549, 574, 586, 590, 609, 611, 614, 623, 632, 643, 692, 699, 709, 737, 755, 759, 772, 783, 784, 808, 817, 830, 864, 867, 872, 891, 894, 898, 900, 913, 917, 919, 934, 939, 944, 960, 964, 974].

460 Kerschensteiner, J. "Beobachtungen zum altsyrischen Acta-text," *Bib* 45/1 (1964): 63-74 [*see also* 060, 237, 358, 367, 377, 378, 490, 511, 537, 578, 698, 789, 827, 862, 896, 908, 910, 914, 926, 955, 970, 977].

461 Kesich, V. "The Apostolic Council at Jerusalem," *SVTQ* 6/3 (1962): 108-17 [*see also* 029, 178, 234, 245, 251, 281, 408, 414, 617, 662, 711, 713, 758, 847, 857].

462 _____. "Resurrection, Ascension, and the Giving of the Spirit," *GOTR* 25 (1980): 249-60 [*see also* 055, 154, 175, 207, 210, 269, 274, 335, 368, 369, 506, 508, 531, 536, 539, 540, 612, 614, 793, 827, 959, 977].

463 Kilgallen, J. J. "Acts: Literary and Theological Turning Points," *BTB* 7 (1977): 177-80.

464 _____. "The Stephen Speech: A Literary and Redactional Study of Acts 7:2-53," *CBQ* 40 (1978): 639 [*see also* 016, 026, 059, 063, 075, 122, 129, 180, 188, 311, 323, 327, 397, 486, 487, 504, 526, 571, 690, 707, 716, 717, 757, 769, 820, 837, 847, 848, 849, 881, 886, 912, 928, 950, 958].

465 _____. "The Unity of Peter's Pentecost Speech," *BibTo* 82 (1976): 650-56 [*see also* 001, 043, 076, 077, 078, 088, 101, 110, 121, 126, 154, 178, 190, 221, 239, 240, 242, 300, 340, 370, 493, 512, 528, 541, 577, 590, 611, 613, 624, 644, 665, 687, 692, 737, 787, 806, 808, 812, 813, 817, 862, 888, 900, 902, 930, 939, 960, 964, 975].

466 Kilpatrick, George D. "Acts 7:56: Son of Man?" *TZ* 21/3 (1965): 209 [*see also* 010, 016, 374, 423, 482, 488, 502, 533, 555, 581, 626, 629, 677, 792, 863, 900, 953].

467 _____. "Acts XXIII. 23 DEXIOLABOI," *JTS* 14/2 (1963): 393-94 [*see also* 088, 390, 436, 451, 674, 700, 868, 924].

468 _____. "Again Acts vii,56: Son of Man?" *TZ* 34/4 (1978): 232 [*see also* 466, 545].

469 _____. "Apollos—Apelles," *JBL* 89/1 (1970): 77.

470 _____. "Eclecticism and Atticism," *ETL* 53 (1977): 107-12.

471 _____. "*Epithyein* and *epikrinein* in the Greek Bible," *ZNW* 74/1-2 (1983): 151-53 [*see also* 180].

472 _____. "A Jewish Background to Acts 2:9-11," *JJS* 26/1-2 (1975): 48-49 [*see also* 035, 736].

473 _____. "The Land of Egypt in the New Testament," *JTS* 17/1 (1966): 70.

474 _____. "*Laoi* at Luke ii. 31 and Acts iv. 25, 27," *JTS* 16 (1965): 127.

475 _____. "The Spirit, God, and Jesus in Acts," *JTS* 15/1 (1964): 63 [*see also* 006, 042, 064, 076, 078, 084, 100, 126, 128, 148, 189, 195, 196, 277, 309, 312, 315, 319, 320, 322, 327, 371, 372, 387, 403, 439, 459, 462, 482, 519, 522, 528, 532, 541, 549, 574, 586, 590, 609, 611, 614, 623, 632, 643, 692, 699, 709, 737, 755, 759, 772, 783, 784, 808, 817, 830, 864, 867, 872, 891, 894, 898, 900, 913, 917, 919, 934, 939, 944, 960, 964, 974].

476 Klawek, Aleksy. "Św. Pawel Przybywa do Europy," *RB* 18/3 (1965): 175-80 [*see also* 047, 069, 151, 155, 156, 163, 166, 280, 329, 615, 841, 949, 984].

477 Klein, G. "Der Synkretismus als theologisches Problem in der ältesten christlichen Apologetik," *ZTK* 64/1 (1967): 40-82.

478 Klein, H. "Zur Frage nach dem Abfassungsort der Lukaschriften," *EvT* 32 (1972): 467-77.

479 Kliesch, K. "Das Heilsgeschichtliche Credo in den Reden der Apostelgeschichte," *BBB* 44 (1975): n.p. [*see also* 194, 430, 835, 947]

480 Klijn, A. F. J. "The Pseudo-Clementines and the Apostolic Decree," *NT* 10/4 (1968): 305-12.

481 Knoch, O. "Erfüllt vom Heiligen Geiste. Die Einheit der Kirche nach der Apostelgeschichte," *BiKi* 18/2 (1963): 34-38.

482 _____. "Jesus, der 'Wohltäter' und 'Befreier' des Menschen. Das Christuszeugnis der Predigt des Petrus vor Kornelius (Apg 10,37f)," *GeL* 46/1 (1973): 1-7 [*see also* 010, 016, 374, 423, 466, 488, 502, 533, 555, 581, 626, 629, 677, 792, 863, 900, 953].

483 Knudsen, Ralph E. "Speaking in Tongues," *F* 9 (1966): 43-57 [*see also* 001, 011, 012, 025, 201, 230, 239, 247, 266, 279, 322, 346, 437, 552, 665, 722, 808, 932, 973, 975].

484 Kodell, J. " 'The Word of God Grew.' The Ecclesial Tendency of *Logos* in Acts 6:7; 12:24; 19:20," *Bib* 55/4 (1974): 505-19 [*see also* 780].

485 Koenig, John. "From Ministry to Ministry: Paul as Interpreter of Charismatic Gifts," *USQR* 33/3-4 (1978): 167-74 [*see also* 580].

486 Koivisto, R. A. "Stephen's Speech: A Case Study in Rhetoric and Biblical Inerrancy," *JETS* 20/4 (1977): 353-64 [*see also* 016, 026, 059, 063, 075, 122, 129, 180, 188, 311, 323, 327, 397, 464, 487, 504, 526, 571, 690, 707, 716, 717, 757, 769, 820, 837, 847, 848, 849, 881, 886, 912, 928, 950, 958].

487 Kopp, Klemens. "Steinigung und Grab des Stephanus," *HLV* 97/2 (1965): 34-41.

488 Korby, P. "Christologie et Baptême à l'Époque du Christianisme Primitif," *NTS* 27 (1981): 270 [*see also* 010, 016, 374, 423, 466, 482, 502, 533, 555, 581, 626, 629, 677, 792, 863, 900, 953].

489 Kosmala, Hans. "Agnostos Theos," *ASTI* 2 (1963): 106-108.

490 Kraft, R. A. "Sahidic Parchment Fragment of Acts 27:4-13 at University Museum, Philadelphia (E 16690 Coptic 1)" *JBL* 94/2 (1975): 256-65 [*see also* 060, 237, 358, 367, 377, 378, 460, 511, 537, 578, 698, 789, 827, 862, 896, 908, 910, 914, 926, 955, 970, 977].

491 Kremer, J. "Les Actes des Apôtres. Traditions, redaction, Theologie," *BETL* 48/1 (1977-1978): 611.

492 _____. "Einfuhrung in die Problematik heutiger Acta-Forschung an hand von Apg 17,10-13," *ETL* 48 (1978): 11-20.

493 _____. "Was geschah Pfingsten? Zur Historizität des Apg 2,1-13 berichteten Pfingstereignisses," *WWa* 28/2 (1973): 192-207 [*see also* 001, 043, 076, 077, 078, 088, 101, 110, 121, 126, 154, 178, 190, 221, 239, 240, 242, 300, 340, 370, 465, 512, 528, 541, 577, 590, 611, 613, 624, 644, 665, 687, 692, 737, 787, 806, 808, 812, 813, 817, 862, 888, 900, 902, 930, 939, 960, 964, 975].

494 Kruse, H. "Das Reich Satans," *Bib* 58/1 (1977): 29-61.

495 Külling, H. "Zur Bedeutung des Agnostos Theos. Eine Exegese zu Apostelgeschichte 17.22.23," *TZ* 36/2 (1980): 65-83.

496 Kümmel, W. G. "Die älteste Form des Aposteldekretes (Act 15, 20, 29)," *Mar* 3 (1965): 278-88.

497 Kurichianil, J. "The Speeches in the Acts and the Old Testament," *ITS* 17/2 (1980): 181-86 [*see also* 070, 096, 115, 193, 199, 326, 554, 647, 839, 846, 867, 921, 968].

498 de Lacey, "D. R. "Paul in Jerusalem," *NTS* 20/1 (1973): 82-86 [*see also* 106, 129, 184, 201, 435, 454, 527, 554, 601, 701, 895].

499 Lach, J. "Katechese über die Kirche von Jerusalem in der Apostelgeschichte (2,42-47); 4,32-35; 5,12-16)," *ColT* 52 (Supplement) (1982): 141-53 [*see also* 198, 289, 356, 454].

500 Lachs, S. T. "The Pharisees and Sadducees on Angels: A Re-Examination of Acts 23:8," *GCJ* 6 (1977): 35-42 [*see also* 024].

501 Ladouceur, D. "Hellenistic Preconceptions of Shipwreck and Pollution, as a Context for Acts 27-28," *HTR* 73 (1980): 435-49 [*see also* 004, 005, 118, 392, 669, 734].

502 Lafferty, Owen J. "Acts 2,14-36: A Study in Christology," *DuR* 6/2 (1966): 235-53 [*see also* 010, 016, 374, 423, 466, 482, 488, 533, 555, 581, 626, 629, 677, 792, 863, 900, 953].

503 Langevin, P.-É. "Les débuts d'un apôtre. Ac 9,26-31," *AssS* 26 (1973): 32-38 [*see also* 035, 100, 148, 167, 178, 232, 323, 372, 504, 564, 609, 661, 739, 760, 777, 784, 812, 850, 854, 869, 870, 890, 895, 941, 971, 984, 987].

504 _____. "Étienne, témoin du Seigneur Jésus. Ac 7,55-60," *AssS* 29 (1973): 19-24 [*see also* 035, 100, 148, 167, 178, 232, 323, 372, 503, 564, 609, 661, 739, 760, 777, 784, 812, 850, 854, 869, 870, 890, 895, 941, 971, 984, 987].

505 LaPointe, R. "Que sont les *kairoi* d'Act 17,26? Etude sémantique et stylistique," *EgT* 3/3 (1972): 323-38 [*see also* 768, 888].

506 LaVerdiere, E. A. "The Ascension of the Risen Lord," *BibTo* 95 (1978): 1553-59 [*see also* 055, 154, 175, 207, 210, 269, 274, 335, 368, 369, 462, 508, 531, 536, 539, 540, 612, 614, 793, 827, 959, 977].

507 Lea, T. D. "How Peter Learned the Old Testament," *SWJT* 22 (1980): 99.

508 Leaney, A. R. C. "Why There Were Forty Days Between Resurrection and the Ascension," *SEv* 4 (1968): 417-19 [*see also* 055, 154, 175, 207, 210, 269, 274, 335, 368, 369, 462, 506, 531, 536, 539, 540, 612, 614, 793, 827, 959, 977].

509 Lebram, J.-C. "Der Aufbau der Areopagrede," *ZNW* 55/3-4 (1964): 221-43 [*see also* 017, 020, 086, 091, 132, 276, 394, 604, 635, 680, 725, 852, 980].

510 _____. "Zwei Bemerkungen zu katechetischen Traditionen in der Apostelgeschichte," *ZNW* 56/3-4 (1965): 203-13.

511 Le Deaut, R. "Actes 7,48 et Matthieu 17,4 (par.) à la lumière du targum palestinien," *RSR* 52/1 (1964): 85-90 [*see also* 060, 237, 358, 367, 377, 378, 460, 490, 537, 578, 698, 789, 827, 862, 896, 908, 910, 914, 926, 955, 970, 977].

512 _____. "Pentecost and Jewish Tradition," *DL* 20/5 (1970): 250-67 [*see also* 003, 021, 133, 296, 308, 355, 445, 551, 569, 632, 703, 777, 801, 810, 897, 927, 928].

513 _____. "Šāvū'ōt och den kristna pingsten i NT," *SEÅ* 44 (1979): 56-59 [*see also* 038, 146, 233, 255, 262, 420, 597, 804, 805, 947].

514 Lee, G. M. "New Testament Gleanings," *Bib* 51/2 (1970): 235-40.

515 _____. "Two Linguistic Parallels from Babrius," *NT* 9/1 (1967): 41-42.

516 Leenhardt, F. J. "Abraham et la Conversion de Saul de Tarse, suivi d'une Note sur 'Abraham Dans Jean 8,' " *RHPR* 53 (1973): 331-51 [*see also* 389, 457, 607, 804, 882].

517 Légasse, S. "L'apologétique à l'égard de Rome dans le procès de Paul. Actes 21,27-26,32," *RSR* 69/2 (1981): 249-55.

518 Legrand, L. "The Areopagus Speech, its Theological Kerygma and its Missionary Significance," *BETL* 41 (1976): (1976): 337-50 [*see also* 091, 098, 132, 197, 231, 286, 394, 509, 577, 635, 725, 728, 730, 852].

519 _____. "The Church in the Acts of the Apostles," *Bhash* 4/2 (1978): 83-97 [*see also* 006, 042, 064, 076, 078, 084, 100, 126, 128, 148, 189, 195, 196, 277, 309, 312, 315, 319, 320, 322, 327, 371, 372, 387, 403, 439, 459, 462, 475, 482, 522, 528, 532, 541, 549, 574, 586, 590, 609, 611, 614, 623, 632, 643, 692, 699, 709, 737, 755, 759, 772, 783, 784, 808, 817, 830, 864, 867, 872, 891, 894, 898, 900, 913, 917, 919, 934, 939, 944, 960, 964, 974].

520 _____. "How Much He Must Suffer for My Name (Acts 9:16)," *ClM* 31/3 (1967): 109-11.

521 _____. "Local Church and Universal Church in the Acts of the Apostles," *Vid* 40/7 (1976): 290-98.

522 _____. "The Spirit, the Mission and the Church: Acts 1:6-8," *Bhash* 8/4 (1982): 204-15 [*see also* 006, 042, 064, 076, 078, 084, 100, 126, 128, 148, 189, 195, 196, 277, 309, 312, 315, 319, 320, 322, 327, 371, 372, 387, 403, 439, 459, 462, 475, 482, 519, 528, 532, 541, 549, 574, 586, 590, 609, 611, 614, 623, 632, 643, 692, 699, 709, 737, 755, 759, 772, 783, 784, 808, 817, 830, 864, 867, 872, 891, 894, 898, 900, 913, 917, 919, 934, 939, 944, 960, 964, 974].

523 _____. "The Structure of Acts 2: The Integral Dimensions of the Charismatic Movement According to Luke," *ITS* 19/3 (1982): 193-209.

524 _____. "The Unknown God of Athens, Acts 17 and the Religion of the Gentiles," *IJT* 30/3-4 (1981): 158-67 [*see also* 144, 363, 382, 427, 449, 538, 683, 701, 774, 782, 935, 944, 969].

525 Lerle, Ernst. "Die Predigt in Lystra (Acta XIV.15-18)," *NTS* 7/1 (1960): 46-55 [*see also* 039, 047, 282, 288, 938].

526 Lienhard, J. T. "Acts 6:1-6: A Redactional View," *CBQ* 37/2 (1975): 228-36 [*see also* 254, 397, 703, 710, 728, 958].

527 Lifshitz, B. "L'origine du nom des Chrétiens," *VC* 16/2 (1962): 65-70 [*see also* 106, 129, 184, 201, 435, 454, 498, 554, 601, 701, 895].

528 Limbeck, M. "Pfingsten: Der Heilige Geist und die Kirche," *LS* 20 (1969): 232-45 [*see also* 006, 042, 064, 076, 078, 084, 100, 126, 128, 148, 189, 195, 196, 277, 309, 312, 315, 319, 320, 322, 327, 371, 372, 387, 403, 439, 459, 462, 475, 482, 519, 522, 532, 541, 549, 574, 586, 590, 609, 611, 614, 623, 632, 643, 692, 699, 709, 737, 755, 759, 772, 783, 784, 808, 817, 830, 864, 867, 872, 891, 894, 898, 900, 913, 917, 919, 934, 939, 944, 960, 964, 974].

529 Lion, Antoine. "Actes et utopies des apôtres et des socialistes," *LVie* 30/153 (1981): 167-73.

530 Lods, Marc. "Argent et magie dans le livre des Actes," *PL* 28/4 (1980): 287-93 [*see also* 007].

531 Lohfink, Gerhard. "Aufgefahren in den Himmel," *GeL* 35/2 (1962): 84-85 [*see also* 055, 154, 175, 207, 210, 269, 274, 335, 368, 369, 462, 506, 508, 536, 539, 540, 612, 614, 793, 827, 959, 977].

532 _____. "Bemerkungen zur neuen Einheitsübersetzung der Bibel. ubersetzungsfehler in der Apostelgeschichte," *TQ* 155/3 (1975): 244-46 [*see also* 006, 042, 064, 076, 078, 084, 100, 126, 128, 148, 189, 195, 196, 277, 309, 312, 315, 319, 320, 322, 327, 371, 372, 387, 403, 439, 459, 462, 475, 482, 519, 522, 528, 541, 549, 574, 586, 590, 609, 611, 614, 623, 632, 643, 692, 699, 709, 737, 755, 759, 772, 783, 784, 808, 817, 830, 864, 867, 872, 891, 894, 898, 900, 913, 917, 919, 934, 939, 944, 960, 964, 974].

533 _____. "Christologie und Geschichtsbild in Apg 3, 19-21," *BZ* (New Series) 13/2 (1969): 223-41 [*see also* 010, 016, 374, 423, 466, 482, 488, 502, 555, 581, 626, 629, 677, 792, 863, 900, 953].

534 _____. "Eine alttestamentliche Darstellungsform für Gotteserscheinungen in den Damaskusberichten (Apg 9;22;26)," *BZ* (New Series) 9/2 (1965): 246-57.

535 _____. "Gibt es noch Taten Gottes?" *Or* 42/11 (1978): 124-26.

536 _____. "Der historische Ansatz der Himmelfahrt Christi," *Cath* 17/1 (1963): 44-84 [*see also* 055, 154, 175, 207, 210, 269, 274, 335, 368, 369, 462, 506, 508, 531, 539, 540, 612, 614, 793, 827, 959, 977].

537 _____. "Ger Losvorgang in Apg 1, 26," *BZ* 19/2 (1975): 248-49 [*see also* 038, 187, 278, 425, 654, 787, 963, 970].

538 _____. "Meinen Namen zu tragen . . . (Apg 9,15)" *BZ* (New Series) 10/1 (1966): 108-15 [*see also* 144, 363, 382, 427, 449, 524, 683, 701, 774, 782, 935, 944, 969].

539 _____. " 'Was steht ihr da und schauet' (Apg 1.11). Die 'Himmelfahrt Jesu' in lukanischen Geschichtswerk," *BiKi* 20/2 (1965): 43-48 [*see also* 055, 154, 175, 207, 210, 269, 274, 335, 368, 369, 462, 506, 508, 531, 536, 540, 612, 614, 793, 827, 959, 977].

540 _____. " 'Wir sind Zeugen dieser Ereignisse' (Apg 5,32). Die Einheit der neutestamentlichen Botschaft von Erhöhung und Himmelfahrt Jesu," *BiKi* 20/2 (1965): 49-52 [*see also* 055, 154, 175, 207, 210, 269, 274, 335, 368, 369, 462, 506, 508, 531, 536, 539, 612, 614, 793, 827, 959, 977].

541 Lohse, E. "Die Bedeutung des Pfingstberichtes im Rahme des lukanischen Geschichtswerkes," *EvT* 13 (1953): 426-36 [*see also* 006, 042, 064, 076, 078, 084, 100, 126, 128, 148, 189, 195, 196, 277, 309, 312, 315, 319, 320, 322, 327, 371, 372, 387, 403, 439, 459, 462, 475, 482, 519, 522, 528, 532, 549, 574, 586, 590, 609, 611, 614, 623, 632, 643, 692, 699, 709, 737, 755, 759, 772, 783, 784, 808, 817, 830, 864, 867, 872, 891, 894, 898, 900, 913, 917, 919, 934, 939, 944, 960, 964, 974].

542 Löning, K. "Die Korneliustradition," *BZ* 18/1 (1974): 1-19 [*see also* 108, 129, 250, 360, 573, 587, 658, 688, 838, 873].

543 _____. "Paulinismus in der Apostelgeschichte," *QD* 89 (1981): 202-31 [*see also* 641].

544 Losada, Diego. "Jesus y Satan," *RBib* 40/169 (1978): 129-46 [*see also* 611].

545 Lovestam, E. "Son and Saviour: A Study of Acts 13:32-37. With an Appendix: 'Son of God' in the Synoptic Gospels," *CNeo* 18 (1961): 5-134 [*see also* 053, 245, 358, 427, 429, 430].

546 de Lubac, H. "De vocations gentium," *RTP* 19/5 (1969): 331-32.

547 Lucchesi, E. "Précédents non bibliques à l'expression néo-testamentaire: 'Les temps et les moments,' " *JTS* 28 (1977): 537-40.

548 Luhrumann, Dieter. "Glaude im frühen Christentum (Mt 11,23; 1 Kor 13,2)," *TL* 103 (1978): 188-91.

549 Lundgren, S. "Ananias and the Calling of Paul in Acts," *ST* 25/2 (1971): 117-22 [*see also* 102, 172, 611, 962].

550 Luz, Hna. "Cristo y la Iglesia, según Hechos," *RBib* 29/4 (1967): 206-23.

551 Lyonnet, S. "La voie' dans les Actes des Apôtres," *RSR* 69/1 (1981): 149-64 [*see also* 003, 021, 133, 296, 308, 355, 445, 512, 569, 632, 703, 777, 801, 810, 897, 927, 928].

552 MacDonald, William G. "Glossolalia in the New Testament," *BETS* 20 (1964): 59-68 [*see also* 001, 011, 012, 025, 201, 230, 239, 247, 266, 279, 322, 346, 437, 483, 665, 722, 808, 932, 973, 975].

553 MacKenzie, R. S. "The Latin Column in Codex Bezae," *JSNT* 6 (1980): 58-76 [*see also* 160, 162, 166, 377, 695, 714, 909].

554 McNulty, T. M. "Pauline Preaching: A Speech-Act Analysis," *W* 53 (1979): 207-14 [*see also* 106, 129, 184, 201, 435, 454, 498, 527, 601, 701, 895].

555 MacRae, G. W. " 'Whom Heaven Must Receive Until the Time.' Reflections on the Christology of Acts," *Int* 27/2 (1973): 151-65 [*see also* 010, 016, 374, 423, 466, 482, 488, 502, 533, 581, 626, 629, 677, 792, 863, 900, 953].

556 Maddox, Robert. "The Purpose of Luke-Acts," *FRL* 126 (1982): 1-218 [*see also* 140, 157, 592].

557 Magass, Walter. "Theologie und Wetterregel. Semiotische Variationen über Arats 'Phainomena,' " *LB* 49 (1981): 7-26.

558 Maier, P. L. "The First Corinthians: Pentecost and the Spread of Christianity," *SB* 8 (1978): 47 [*see also* 136, 149, 200, 295, 359, 518, 522, 538, 591, 646, 683, 703, 848, 905, 961].

559 Maisch, I. "Dienst am Wort und für die Tische. Vier Worte aus der Apostelgeschichte zum kirchlichen Dienst," *BibLeb* 10/1 (1969): 83-87 [*see also* 173, 176, 332, 336, 567, 654, 687, 763].

560 Malherbe, A. J. "The Apologetic Theology of the Preaching Peter," *RQ* 13 (1970): 205-23 [*see also* 030, 216, 234, 240, 465].

561 Maly, Karl. "Apostolische Gemeindeführung," *TG* 10 (1967): 219-22.

562 Mánek, Jindřich. "Das Aposteldekret im Kontext der Lukastheologie," *CV* 15/2 (1972): 151-60.

563 _____. "Vier Bibelstudien zur Problematik der sozialen Umwandlung," *CV* 10/1 (1967): 61-70; 10/2-3 (1967): 179-82 [*see also* 206, 213, 401, 457, 621, 670, 691, 873, 874, 906].

564 Mangatt, G. "The Acts of the Apostles: An Introduction," *Bhash* 4/2 (1978): 75-82 [*see also* 035, 100, 148, 167, 178, 232, 323, 372, 503, 504, 609, 661, 739, 760, 777, 784, 812, 850, 854, 869, 870, 890, 895, 941, 971, 984, 987].

565 _____. "The Pentecostal Gift of the Spirit," *BiBe* 2 (1976): 227-39, 300-14.

566 Manns, Frédéric. "Essais sur le Judeo-Christianisme," *RBib* 27 (1979): 433-37.

567 _____. ''Un midrash chrétien: le récit de la mort de Judas,''
     RScR 54/3 (1980): 197-203 [*see also* 173, 176, 332, 336, 559,
     654, 687, 763].

568 _____. ''Remarques sur Actes 15,20.29,'' *Anton* 53/3-4
     (1978):443-51.

569 Manzanera, M. ''Koinonia en Hch 2,42. Notas sobre su inter-
     pretación y origen historico-doctrinal,'' *EE* 52/202 (1977):
     307-29 [*see also* 003, 021, 133, 296, 308, 355, 445, 512,
     551, 632, 703, 777, 801, 810, 897, 927, 928].

570 Marco, A. ''Di, Der Chiasmus in der Bibel IV. Apg. Apk; Erste
     Schlussfolgerungen,'' *LB* 44 (1979): 3-70.

571 Mare, W. H. ''Acts 7: Jewish or Samaritan in Character?'' *WTJ*
     34/1 (1971): 1-21 [*see also* 016, 026, 059, 063, 075, 122,
     129, 180, 188, 311, 323, 327, 397, 464, 486, 487, 504, 526,
     690, 707, 716, 717, 757, 769, 820, 837, 847, 848, 849, 881,
     886, 912, 928, 950, 958].

572 _____. ''Pauline Appeals to Historical Evidence,'' *Bull-
     BETS* 11/3 (1968): 121-30.

573 Marin, Louis. ''Essai d'analyse structurale d'Actes 10,1-11,18,''
     RSR 58/1 (1970): 39-61 [*see also* 108, 129, 250, 360, 542,
     587, 658, 688, 838, 873].

574 Marsh, Thomas. ''Holy Spirit in Early Christian Teaching,'' *ITQ*
     45/2 (1978): 101-16 [*see also* 006, 042, 064, 076, 078, 084,
     100, 126, 128, 148, 189, 195, 196, 277, 309, 312, 315, 319,
     320, 322, 327, 371, 372, 387, 403, 439, 459, 462, 475, 482,
     519, 522, 528, 532, 541, 549, 586, 590, 609, 611, 614, 623,
     632, 643, 692, 699, 709, 737, 755, 759, 772, 783, 784, 808,
     817, 830, 864, 867, 872, 891, 894, 898, 900, 913, 917, 919,
     934, 939, 944, 960, 964, 974].

575 Marshall, I. Howard. ''La comunicazione dell'Evvangelo al
     mondo non cristiano nel NT,'' *STE* 2/3 (1979): 37-76.

576 _____. ''Recent Study of the Acts of the Apostles,'' *ET* 80/
     10 (1969): 292-96 [*see also* 067, 082, 303, 304, 341, 357,
     409].

577 _____. "The Significance of Pentecost," *SJT* 30 (1977): 347-69 [*see also* 091, 098, 132, 197, 231, 286, 394, 509, 518, 635, 725, 728, 730, 852].

578 Martin, R. A. "Syntactical Evidence of Aramaic Sources in Acts i-xv," *NTS* 11/1 (1964-1965): 38-59 [*see also* 169, 985].

579 Martini, Carlo M. "L'esclusione dalla comunità del popolo di Dio e il nuovo Israele secondo Atti 3,23," *Bib* 50/1 (1969): 1-14.

580 _____. "Ministères et entraide fraternelle dans la communauté primitive (Ac 6)," *AS* (New Series) 26 (1973): 4-11 [*see also* 485].

581 _____. "Riflessioni sulla cristologia degli Atti," *SacD* 16/63-64 (1971): 525-34 [*see also* 010, 016, 374, 423, 466, 482, 488, 502, 533, 555, 626, 629, 677, 792, 863, 900, 953].

582 Marx, W. G. "A New Theophilus," *EQ* 52 (1980): 17-26 [*see also* 092, 619].

583 Marzotto, Damiano. "L'unita degle uomini nel vangelo di Giovanni," *ETR* 54 (1979): 641.

584 Mascialino, Miguel. "¿Como se está estudéando el libro de los Hechos de los Apóstoles en la actualidad?" *RBib* 24 (1962): 51.

585 Masini, M. "La testimonianza cristiana, spunti dal libro degli atti," *Ser* 2/6 (1968): 165-84 [*see also* 368, 916].

586 Massó, R. "La promesa del Espíritu (Hechos 8,5-8, 14-17; 1 Pe 3,15-18; Jn 14,15-21)" *CuBi* 29 (1972): 342-48 [*see also* 006, 042, 064, 076, 078, 084, 100, 126, 128, 148, 189, 195, 196, 277, 309, 312, 315, 319, 320, 322, 327, 371, 372, 387, 403, 439, 459, 462, 475, 482, 519, 522, 528, 532, 541, 549, 574, 590, 609, 611, 614, 623, 632, 643, 692, 699, 709, 737, 755, 759, 772, 783, 784, 808, 817, 830, 864, 867, 872, 891, 894, 898, 900, 913, 917, 919, 934, 939, 944, 960, 964, 974].

587 Masson, C. "A propos de Act. 9.19b-25. Note sur l'utilisation de Gal. et de 2 Cor. par l'auteur des Actes," *TZ* 18/3 (1962): 161-66 [*see also* 108, 129, 250, 360, 542, 573, 587, 688, 838, 873].

588 Mastin, B. A. "A Note on Acts 19,14," *Bib* 59/1 (1978): 97-99.

589 —————. "Scaeva the Chief Priest," *JTS* 27/2 (1976): 405-12.

590 Matta-El-Meskin, P. "La Pentecôte," *Ir* 50/1 (1977): 5-45 [*see also* 006, 042, 064, 076, 078, 084, 100, 126, 128, 148, 189, 195, 196, 277, 309, 312, 315, 319, 320, 322, 327, 371, 372, 387, 403, 439, 459, 462, 475, 482, 519, 522, 528, 532, 541, 549, 574, 586, 609, 611, 614, 623, 632, 643, 692, 699, 709, 737, 755, 759, 772, 783, 784, 808, 817, 830, 864, 867, 872, 891, 894, 898, 900, 913, 917, 919, 934, 939, 944, 960, 964, 974].

591 Matthey, J. "La mission de l'église au temps des apôtres et au temps de Luc," *LV* 30/153-54 (1981): 61-71 [*see also* 136, 149, 200, 295, 359, 518, 522, 538, 558, 646, 683, 703, 848, 905, 961].

592 Mattill, A. J. "The Jesus-Paul Parallels and the Purpose of Luke-Acts: H. H. Evans Reconsidered," *NT* 17 (1975): 15-46 [*see also* 140, 157, 556].

593 —————. "Naherwartung, Fernerwartung, and the Purpose of Luke-Acts: Weymouth Reconsidered," *CBQ* 34/3 (1972): 276-93 [*see also* 258, 268, 294, 318, 319, 383, 402, 919, 941].

594 —————. "The Value of Acts as a Source for the Study of Paul," *PRS* 5 (1978): 76-98.

595 Matute, A. "La puerta de la fe (Act 14,21-28)" *Hel* 21 (1970): 421-39.

596 Mealand, D. L. "Community of Goods and Utopian Allusions in Acts II-IV," *JTS* 28/1 (1977): 96-99.

597 —————. "Community of Goods at Qumran," *TZ* 31 (1975): 129-39 [*see also* 038, 146, 233, 255, 262, 420, 513, 804, 805, 947].

598 Mecham, F. A. "And So We Came to Rome," *ACR* 50/2 (1973): 170-73 [*see also* 323, 472, 564, 694, 735, 741, 784, 825, 869, 941, 965].

599 Meeks, W. A. "Die Funktion des vom Himmel hierabgestiegenen Offenbarers für das Selbstzeugnis der johannischen Gemeinde," *JBL* 92 (1972): 44-72.

600 _____. "Simon Magus in Recent Research," *RelSR* 3/3 (1977): 137-42.

601 van der Meer, W. "Informatieve kanttekeningen bij een methode van exegese Der Beitrag der strukturalen Analyse zur Exegese von Apg 10,1ff.," *GTT* 75/4 (1975): 193-206 [*see also* 106, 129, 184, 201, 435, 454, 498, 527, 554, 701, 895].

602 de Meester, P. "Le pèlerin d'Éthiopie. Essai d'une interprétation 'africaine' des Actes 8,26-40," *Tel* 18 (1979): 5-18 [*see also* 129, 134, 139, 270, 306, 603, 622, 681].

603 _____. " 'Philippe et l'eunuque éthiopien' ou 'Le baptême d'un pèlerin de Nubie'?" *NRT* 103/3 (1981): 360-74 [*see also* 152, 196, 270, 315, 324, 448, 488, 673, 699, 817, 907, 974].

604 Meinardus, O. F. A. "An Athenian Tradition: St. Paul's Refuge in the Well," *OKS* 21/2-3 (1972): 181-86 [*see also* 017, 020, 086, 091, 132, 276, 394, 509, 635, 680, 725, 852, 980].

605 _____. "Melita Illyrica or Africana: An Examination of the Site of St. Paul's Shipwreck," *OS* 23/1 (1974): 21-36 [*see also* 001, 392].

606 _____. "St. Paul Shipwrecked in Dalmatia," *BA* 39/4 (1976): 145-47.

607 _____. "The Site of the Apostle Paul's Conversion at Kaukab," *BA* 44/1 (1981): 57-59 [*see also* 389, 457, 516, 804, 882].

608 Menestrina, G. "*Aphixis*," *BibO* 20/1 (1978): 50.

609 Menoud, P.-H. "La Pentecôte lucanienne et l'histoire," *RHPR* 42/2-3 (1962): 141-47 [*see also* 006, 042, 064, 076, 078, 084, 100, 126, 128, 148, 189, 195, 196, 277, 309, 312, 315, 319, 320, 322, 327, 371, 372, 387, 403, 439, 459, 462, 475, 482, 519, 522, 528, 532, 541, 549, 574, 586, 590, 611, 614, 623, 632, 643, 692, 699, 709, 737, 755, 759, 772, 783, 784, 808, 817, 830, 864, 867, 872, 891, 894, 898, 900, 913, 917, 919, 934, 939, 944, 960, 964, 974].

610 Merrill, E. H. "Paul's Use of 'About 450 Years' in Acts 13:20," *BS* 138/551 (1981): 246-57.

611 Mettayer, A. "Ambiguïté et terrorisms du sacré: Analyse d'un texte des Actes des Apôtres (4,31-5,111)," *SR* 7/4 (1978): 415-24 [*see also* 102, 172, 549, 962].

612 Metzger, B. M. "The Meaning of Christ's Ascension," *ChrTo* 10 (May 10, 1966): 863-64 [*see also* 055, 154, 175, 207, 210, 269, 274, 335, 368, 369, 462, 506, 508, 531, 536, 539, 540, 614, 793, 827, 959, 977].

613 Meyer, B. F. "The Meaning of Pentecost," *W* 40/5 (1966): 281-87 [*see also* 001, 043, 076, 077, 078, 088, 101, 110, 121, 126, 154, 178, 190, 221, 239, 240, 242, 300, 340, 370, 465, 493, 512, 528, 541, 577, 590, 611, 624, 644, 665, 687, 692, 737, 787, 806, 808, 812, 813, 817, 862, 888, 900, 902, 930, 939, 960, 964, 975].

614 Michiels, R. "Eenheid van Pasen, Hemelvaart en Pinksteren," *Col* 20/1 (1974): 3-35 [*see also* 055, 154, 175, 207, 210, 269, 274, 335, 368, 369, 462, 506, 508, 531, 536, 539, 540, 612, 793, 827, 959, 977].

615 Miesner, Donald R. "The Missionary Journeys Narrative: Patterns and Implications," *PRS* 5 (1978): 199-214 [*see also* 047, 069, 151, 155, 156, 163, 166, 280, 329, 476, 841, 949, 984].

616 Miguens, M. "Appunti sull'esegesi dell'epoca apostolica," *BibO* 3/6 (1961): 201-206.

617 _____. "Pietro nel conciglio apostòlico," *RBib* 10/3 (1962): 240-51 [*see also* 029, 178, 234, 245, 251, 281, 408, 414, 461, 662, 711, 713, 758, 847, 857].

618 Miles, G. B. and G. Trompf. "Luke and Antiphon: The Theology of Acts 27-28 in the Light of Pagan Beliefs About Divine Retribution, Pollution, and Shipwreck," *HTR* 69/3-4 (1976): 259-67 [*see also* 605, 669, 818].

619 Minear, P. S. "Dear Theo. The Kerygmatic Intention and Claim of the Book of Acts," *Int* 27/2 (1973): 131-50 [*see also* 092, 120, 342, 453, 518, 582, 852, 952].

620 Miquel, Pierre. "Christ's Ascension and Our Glorification," *TD* 9 (1961): 67-73.

621 Mínguez, D. "Estructura dinámica de la conversión. Reflexión sobre Hch 2,38-39," *EE* 54/210 (1979): 383-94 [*see also* 206, 213, 401, 457, 563, 670, 691, 873, 874, 906].

622 _____. "Hechos 8,25-40. Análisis estructural del relato," *Bib* 57/2 (1976): 168-91 [*see also* 129, 134, 139, 270, 306, 602, 603, 681].

623 _____. "Hechos de los Apóstoles. Comunidad de creyentes Impulsados por el Espíritu," *SalT* 65/1-2 (1975): 106-13 [*see also* 006, 042, 064, 076, 078, 084, 100, 126, 128, 148, 189, 195, 196, 277, 309, 312, 315, 319, 320, 322, 327, 371, 372, 387, 403, 439, 459, 462, 475, 482, 519, 522, 528, 532, 541, 549, 574, 586, 590, 609, 611, 614, 632, 643, 692, 699, 709, 737, 755, 759, 772, 783, 784, 808, 817, 830, 864, 867, 872, 891, 894, 898, 900, 913, 917, 919, 934, 939, 944, 960, 964, 974].

624 _____. "Pentecostes. Ensayo de semiotica narrativa en Hch," *CBQ* 40 (1978): 643 [*see also* 001, 043, 076, 077, 078, 088, 101, 110, 121, 126, 154, 178, 190, 221, 239, 240, 242, 300, 340, 370, 465, 493, 512, 528, 541, 577, 590, 611, 613, 644, 665, 687, 692, 737, 787, 806, 808, 812, 813, 817, 862, 888, 900, 902, 930, 939, 960, 964, 975].

625 Misiurek, J. "Emaus (Lk 24,13-36)," *RBL* 31 (1978): 240-46 [*see also* 134, 306, 343].

626 Mlotek, Antoni. "De S. Scriptura in vita primorum christiano-rum," *RBL* 30 (1977): 310-23 [*see also* 010, 016, 374, 423, 466, 482, 488, 502, 533, 555, 581, 629, 677, 792, 863, 900, 953].

627 _____. "La Vita spirituale dei primi cristiani e la lettura della Bibbia," *SacD* 24 (1979): 439-48.

628 Moellering, H. A. "Deisidaimonia: A Footnote to Acts 17:22," *CTM* 34/8 (1963): 466-71.

629 Montague, G. T. "Paul and Athens," *BibTo* 49 (1970): 14-23 [*see also* 010, 016, 374, 423, 466, 482, 488, 502, 533, 555, 581, 626, 677, 792, 863, 900, 953].

630 del Moral, A. García. "Disciplina y pastoral en el Libro de los Hechos, al narrar el itinerario paulino. La vida eclesial de San Pablo, presupuesto y contexto de sus cartas," *Com* 15/3 (1982): 319-92.

631 _____. "Un posible aspecto de la tesis y unidad del libro de los Hechos," *EB* 23/1 (1964): 41-92.

632 de Morales, M. V. Gómez. "La comunidad primitiva modelo de consagración a Dios," *BibFe* 4/12 (1978): 271-82 [*see also* 003, 021, 133, 296, 308, 355, 445, 512, 551, 569, 703, 777, 801, 810, 897, 927, 928].

633 Morel, B. "Eutychus et les fondements Bibliques du Culte," *ETR* 37/1 (1962): 41-47 [*see also* 965].

634 Moretti, A. "Mi sarete testimoni (Atti 1,8)" *PV* 15 (1970): 421-36.

635 Morrice, W. G. "Where Did Paul Speak in Athens—On Mars' Hill or Before the Court of the Areopagus?" *ET* 83/12 (1972): 377-78 [*see also* 017, 020, 086, 091, 132, 276, 394, 509, 604, 680, 725, 852, 980].

636 Moulton, H. K. "Acts 2:22: Jesus . . . A Man Approved by God?" *BiTr* 30 (1979): 344-45.

637 Moxnes, H. "Fra jødisk sekt till verdensreligion. Adolf von Harnack og plaseringen av Lukas-Acta innenfor urkristendommens utvikling," *NTTid* 73/3-4 (1972): 229-55 [*see also* 314, 782, 820, 912].

638 Mulder, H. "Barnabas en de gemeente te Jeruzalem," *HB* 24 (1965): 195-200 [*see also* 245, 267, 282, 288, 330, 347, 653, 749, 895]

639 _____. "Jacobus, leider van de gemeente te Jeruzalem (holl)" *HB* 23/8 (1964): 184-89.

640 Müller, P.-G. "Die 'Bekehrung' des Petrus. Zur Interpretation von Apg 10,1-11,18," *HK* 28/7 (1974): 372-75 [*see also* 050, 107, 162, 176, 181, 219, 245, 250, 252, 328, 414, 498, 645, 658, 672, 711, 785, 787, 815, 942, 964, 965].

641 _____. "Der 'Paulinismus' in der Apostelgeschichte. Ein forschungsgeschichtlicher überblick," *QD* 89 (1981): 157-201 [*see also* 543].

642 Muller, U. B. "Zur Rezeption Gesetzeskritischer Jesusüberlieferung im frühen Christentum," *NTS* 27 (1981): 163-67.

643 Mulligan, J. E. "I Shall Put My Spirit in You," *CCr* 20/2 (1968): 201-10 [*see also* 006, 042, 064, 076, 078, 084, 100, 126, 128, 148, 189, 195, 196, 277, 309, 312, 315, 319, 320, 322, 327, 371, 372, 387, 403, 439, 459, 462, 475, 482, 519, 522, 528, 532, 541, 549, 574, 586, 590, 609, 611, 614, 623, 632, 692, 699, 709, 737, 755, 759, 772, 783, 784, 808, 817, 830, 864, 867, 872, 891, 894, 898, 900, 913, 917, 919, 934, 939, 944, 960, 964, 974].

644 Mussner, F. "In den Letzten Tagen (Apg 2, 17a)" *BZ* 5/2 (1961): 263-65 [*see also* 001, 043, 076, 077, 078, 088, 101, 110, 121, 126, 154, 178, 190, 221, 239, 240, 242, 300, 340, 370, 465, 493, 512, 528, 541, 577, 590, 611, 613, 624, 665, 687, 692, 737, 787, 806, 808, 812, 813, 817, 862, 888, 900, 902, 930, 939, 960, 964, 975].

645 ————. "Petrus und Paulus' Pole der Einheit 1976," *CC* 129 (1978): 615 [*see also* 044, 089, 180, 252, 288, 653, 661, 708, 795, 815, 877, 893, 942, 980].

646 Nagy, St. "Hierarchia koscielna w okresie misyjnej dzialalnosci sw. Pawla," *RTK* 11/2 (1964): 55-79 [*see also* 136, 149, 200, 295, 359, 518, 522, 538, 558, 591, 683, 703, 848, 905, 961].

647 Navone, J. "Speeches in Acts," *BibTo* 65 (1973): 1114-17 [*see also* 055, 226, 227, 320, 644].

648 Neirynck, F. "Acts 10:63a τὸν λόγον ὄν," *ETL* 60/1 (1984): 118-23.

649 ————. "Apêlthen pròs heautón (Lc 24,12 et Jn 20,10)," *ETL* 54 (1978): 104-18.

650 ————. "Le Livre des Actes (6): Ac 10:36-43 et l'Évangile," *ETL* 60/1 (1984): 109-17.

651 ————. "Le Livre des Actes dans les récents commentaires," *ETL* 59/4 (1983): 338-49.

652 ————. "Note sur le texte occidental des Actes," *ETL* 58/1 (1982): 105.

653 Nellessen, E. "Die Einsetzung von Presbytern durch Barnabas und Paulus (Apg 14,23)," *BBB* 53 (1980): 175-93 [*see also* 245, 267, 282, 288, 330, 347, 638, 749, 895].

654 _____. "Tradition und Schrift in der Perikope von der Erwählung des Mattias (Apg 1,15-26)" *BZ* 19/2 (1975): 205-18 [*see also* 173, 176, 332, 336, 559, 567, 687, 763].

655 Nestle, E. "Act 17,11," *ZNW* 15 (1914): 91-92.

656 Nibley, H. "Evangelium Quadraginta Dierum," *VC* 20/1 (1966): 1-24.

657 Noack, Bent. "Si passibilis Christus (Acta 26,33)," *SEÅ* 37/38 (1972-1973): 211-21.

658 Nolland, J. L. "A Fresh Look at Acts 15:10," *NTS* 27/1 (1980): 105-15 [*see also* 108, 129, 250, 360, 542, 573, 587, 688, 838, 873].

659 North, J. L. "Is ΙΔΕΙΝ ΠΕΡΙ (Acts 15,6 cf. 18,15) a Latinism?" *NTS* 29/2 (1983): 264-66.

660 _____. "Μάρκος ὁ κολοβοδάκτυλος: Hippolytus, Elenchus, VII.30," *JTS* 28/2 (1977): 498-507.

661 Nunez, M. de Burgos. "La comunidad de Antioquia: Aspèctos historicos y papel profético en los origenes del cristianismo," *IKZ* 15/1 (1982): 3-26 [*see also* 035, 100, 148, 167, 178, 232, 323, 372, 503, 504, 564, 609, 739, 760, 777, 784, 812, 850, 854, 869, 870, 890, 895, 941, 971, 984, 987].

662 _____. "Opcíon profética ý pluralismo teológico en la eclesiología de los Hechos de los Apóstoles," *Com* 13/2 (1980): 151-95 [*see also* 029, 178, 234, 245, 251, 281, 408, 414, 461, 617, 711, 713, 758, 847, 857].

663 O'Callaghan, J. "Nuevo pergamino de la Vulgate latina (Act 10,23-48)" *Bib* 56/3 (1975): 410-15.

664 Ogg, G. "Derbe," *NTS* 9/4 (1963): 367-70.

665 O'Hagan, A. P. "The First Christian Pentecost (Acts 2:1-13),"
SBFLA 23 (1973): 50-66 [*see also* 001, 043, 076, 077, 078,
088, 101, 110, 121, 126, 154, 178, 190, 221, 239, 240, 242,
300, 340, 370, 465, 493, 512, 528, 541, 577, 590, 611, 613,
624, 644, 687, 692, 737, 787, 806, 808, 812, 813, 817, 862,
888, 900, 902, 930, 939, 960, 964, 975].

666 Ordon, Hubert. "Cezarejska decyzia Piotra. Rozwazania li-
trackoteologiczne nad perydopa o chrzcie Korneliusza: Dz
10,1-11,18," *Sum* 7 (1978): 51-68.

667 O'Reilly, L. "Chiastic Structures in Acts 1-7," *PIBA* 7 (1983):
87-103.

668 Orlett, R. "The Breaking of Bread in Acts," *BibTo* 1/2 (1962):
108-13.

669 Orr, R. W. "Paul's Voyage and Shipwreck," *EQ* 35/2 (1963):
103-104 [*see also* 004, 005, 118, 392, 501, 734].

670 Ory, Georges. "La 'conversion' de Simon le magicien," *CahC*
3/9 (1965): 1-16 [*see also* 008, 037, 048, 174, 365, 799, 868].

671 _____. "Interpolations du Nouveau Testament: II. Le Livre
des Actes," *CahC* 10/33 (1962): 1-40.

672 Osborne, R. E. "Where Did Peter Go?" *CanJT* 14/4 (1968): 274-
77 [*see also* 001, 705, 892].

673 Osburn, C. D. "The Third Person Imperative in Acts 2:38," *RQ*
26/2 (1983): 81-84 [*see also* 152, 196, 270, 315, 324, 448,
488, 603, 699, 817, 907, 974].

674 Oster, R. "The Ephesian Artemis as an Opponent of Early
Christianity," *JAC* 19 (1976): 30-44 [*see also* 088, 390, 436,
451, 467, 700, 868, 924].

675 O'Toole, R. F. "Activity of the Risen Jesus in Luke-Acts," *Bib*
62/4 (1981): 471-98 [*see also* 024, 055, 058, 077, 142, 168,
223, 334, 343, 363, 386, 458, 462, 506, 508, 609, 678, 683,
756, 763, 803, 832, 862, 950].

676 _____. "Acts 2:30 and the Davidic Covenant of Pentecost," *JBL* 102/2 (1983): 245-58.

677 _____. "Acts 26, The Christological Climax of Paul's Defense," *TL* 104 (1979): 825 [*see also* 010, 016, 374, 423, 466,
482, 488, 502, 533, 555, 581, 626, 629, 792, 863, 900, 953].

678 _____. ''Christ's Resurrection in Acts 13:13-52,'' *Bib* 160/
3 (1979): 361-72 [*see also* 086, 091, 098, 217, 218, 243, 431,
432, 554, 725, 852].

679 _____. ''Luke's Notion of 'Be Imitators of Me as I am of
Christ' in Acts 25-26,'' *BibTB* 8/4 (1978): 155-61 [*see also*
209, 819].

680 _____. ''Paul at Athens and Luke's Notion of Worship,''
RBib 89/2 (1982): 185-97 [*see also* 017, 020, 086, 091, 132,
276, 394, 509, 604, 635, 725, 852, 980].

681 _____. ''Philip and the Ethiopian Eunuch (Acts VIII, 25-
40),'' *JSNT* 17 (1983): 25-34 [*see also* 129, 134, 139, 270,
306, 602, 603, 622].

682 _____. ''Some Observations on *anistēmi,* 'I Raise,' in Acts
3:22-26,'' *SE* 31/1 (1978): 84-92.

683 _____. ''Why Did Luke Write Acts (Lk-Acts)?'' *BibTB* 7/
2 (1977): 66-76 [*see also* 144, 363, 382, 427, 449, 524, 538,
701, 774, 782, 935, 944, 969].

684 Panagopoulos, Johannes. ''Die Apostelgeschichte und ihre kritische Untersuchung (neugr.)'' *Teo* 42 (1972): 350-368, 682-
691.

685 _____. ''Zur Theologie der Apostelgeschichte,'' *NT* 14/2
(1972): 137-59.

686 Panier, L. ''Comprenez pourquoi vous comprenez! Actes 1,15-
2,47,'' *SémBib* 23 (1981): 20-43.

687 _____. ''La mort de Judas. Éléments d'analyse sémiotique
du récit de la pentecôte,'' *LV* 30/153-54 (1981): 111-22 [*see
also* 173, 176, 332, 336, 559, 567, 654, 763].

688 _____. ''Parcours pour lire les Actes des Apôtres,'' *SémB*
32 (1983): 27-32 [*see also* 108, 129, 250, 360, 542, 573, 587,
658, 838, 873].

689 _____. ''Pour lire les Actes des Apôtres. 2e partie: les chap-
itres 3-5,'' *SémB* 29 (1983): 11-18 [*see also* 057, 059, 461,
885, 914].

690 _____. "Pour lire les Actes des Apôtres. 3e série: Ac. 6-9," *SémB* 30 (1983): 34-42 [*see also* 037, 063, 109, 174, 208, 270, 602, 603, 681, 800].

691 Panimolle, S. A. "La charis negli Atti e nel quarto vangelo," *RBib* 25/2 (1977): 143-58 [*see also* 206, 213, 401, 457, 563, 621, 670, 873, 874, 906].

692 Papa, Benigno. "L'effusione dello spirito a Pentecoste," *PSV* 4 (1981): 142-59 [*see also* 006, 042, 064, 076, 078, 084, 100, 126, 128, 148, 189, 195, 196, 277, 309, 312, 315, 319, 320, 322, 327, 371, 372, 387, 403, 439, 459, 462, 475, 482, 519, 522, 528, 532, 541, 549, 574, 586, 590, 609, 611, 614, 623, 632, 643, 699, 709, 737, 755, 759, 772, 783, 784, 808, 817, 830, 864, 867, 872, 891, 894, 898, 900, 913, 917, 919, 934, 939, 944, 960, 964, 974].

693 _____. "Tensioni e unita della Chiesa. Ricerca storico-teologica negli Atti degli Apostoli," *ETR* 53 (1978): 136

694 Parisi, G. "Il luogo della biennale dimora paolina in Roma," *PC* 40 (November 1, 1961): 1145-55; 40 (November 15, 1961): 1203-12; 40 (December 1, 1961): 1264-75 [*see also* 323, 472, 564, 598, 735, 741, 784, 825, 869, 941, 965].

695 Parker, D. "A 'Dictation Theory' of Codex Bezae," *JSNT* 15 (1982): 97-112 [*see also* 160, 162, 166, 377, 553, 714, 909].

696 Parker, Pierson. "The 'Former Treatise' and the Date of Acts," *JBL* 84/1 (1965): 52-58.

697 _____. "Once More, Acts and Galatians," *JBL* 86/2 (1967): 1975-82.

698 _____. "Three Variant Readings in Luke-Acts," *JBL* 83 (1964): 165-70 [*see also* 060, 237, 358, 367, 377, 378, 460, 490, 511, 537, 578, 789, 827, 862, 896, 908, 910, 914, 926, 955, 970, 977].

699 Parratt, J. K. "The Holy Spirit and Baptism. Part I. The Gospels and the Acts of the Apostles," *ET* 82/8 (1971): 231-35 [*see also* 152, 196, 270, 315, 324, 448, 488, 603, 673, 817, 907, 974].

700 _____. "The Repabtism of the Ephesian Disciples," *ET* 79/6 (1968): 182-83 [*see also* 090, 243, 448].

701 Pasinya, Monsengwo. "Antioche, berceau de l'Eglise des Gentils? Act 11,19-26," *RAT* 1/1 (1977): 31-66 [*see also* 106, 129, 184, 201, 435, 454, 498, 527, 554, 601, 895].

702 Pathrapankal, J. "Creative Crises of Leadership in the Acts of the Apostles," *IJT* 32/12 (1983): 52-60.

703 ⸻. "The Hellenists and Their Missionary Dynamism in the Early Church and its Message for Our Times," *Bhash* 8/4 (1982): 216-26 [*see also* 003, 021, 133, 296, 308, 355, 445, 512, 551, 569, 632, 777, 801, 810, 897, 927, 928].

704 Patsch, H. "Die Prophetie des Agabus," *TZ* 28 (1972): 228-32.

705 Paul, A. "Le Christianisme Primitif. Diaspora, Dissemination et exclusion," *LVie* 141 (1979): 5-16 [*see also* 001, 672, 892].

706 Pelletier, André. "Une création de l'apologétique chrétienne: *moschopoiein*," *RSR* 54/3 (1966): 411-16.

707 ⸻. "Valeur évocatrice d'un démarquage chrétien de la Septante," *Bib* 48/3 (1967): 388-94 [*see also* 016, 026, 059, 063, 075, 122, 129, 180, 188, 311, 323, 327, 397, 464, 486, 487, 504, 526, 571, 690, 716, 717, 757, 769, 820, 837, 847, 848, 849, 881, 886, 912, 928, 950, 958].

708 Pelser, G. M. M. "The Apostolic Synod—Luke and Paul: A Comparison (Afrikaans)" *HTS* 34 (n.d.): 81-90 [*see also* 044, 089, 180, 252, 288, 645, 653, 661, 795, 815, 877, 893, 942, 980].

709 Penna, Romano. "Lo 'Spirito di Gesù' in *Atti* 16,7. Analisi letteraria e Teologica," *RBib* 20/3 (1972): 241-61 [*see also* 006, 042, 064, 076, 078, 084, 100, 126, 128, 148, 189, 195, 196, 277, 309, 312, 315, 319, 320, 322, 327, 371, 372, 387, 403, 439, 459, 462, 475, 482, 519, 522, 528, 532, 541, 549, 574, 586, 590, 609, 611, 614, 623, 632, 643, 692, 699, 737, 755, 759, 772, 783, 784, 808, 817, 830, 864, 867, 872, 891, 894, 898, 900, 913, 917, 919, 934, 939, 944, 960, 964, 974].

710 Pereira, F. "Persecution in Acts," *Bhash* 4/2 (1978): 131-55 [*see also* 254, 526, 958].

711 Peretto, L. "Pietro e Paolo e l'anno 49 nella complessa situ-azione palestinese," *RBib* 15/3 (1967): 295-308 [*see also* 029, 178, 234, 245, 251, 281, 408, 414, 461, 617, 662, 713, 758, 847, 857].

712 Perrin, N. "The Evangelist as Author: Reflections on Method in the Study and Interpretation of the Synoptic Gospels and Acts," *BiR* 17 (1972): 5-18.

713 Perrot, C. "The Decrees of the Council of Jerusalem," *TD* 30/1 (1982): 21-24 [*see also* 029, 178, 234, 245, 251, 281, 408, 414, 461, 617, 662, 711, 758, 847, 857].

714 _____. "Un fragment christo-palestinien découvert à Khirbet Mird (Act., X, 28-29; 32-41)" *RBib* 70-4 (1963): 506-55 [*see also* 160, 162, 166, 377, 553, 695, 909].

715 Pesch, Rudolph. "Der Anfang der Apostelgeschichte: Apg 1,1-11. Kommentarstudie," *EKK* 3 (1971): 7-35.

716 _____. "Der Christ als Nachahmer Christi. Der Tod des Stephanus (Apg 7) im Vergleich mit dem Tode Christi," *BiKi* 24/1 (1969): 10-11 [*see also* 016, 026, 059, 063, 075, 122, 129, 180, 188, 311, 323, 327, 397, 464, 486, 487, 504, 526, 571, 690, 707, 717, 757, 769, 820, 837, 847, 848, 849, 881, 886, 912, 928, 950, 958].

717 _____. "Die Vision des Stephanus Apg 7,55f. im Rahmen der Apostelgeschichte," *BibLeb* 6/2 (1965): 92-107; 6/3 (1965): 170-83.

718 Pesch, R., E. Gerhart, and F. Schilling. " 'Hellenisten' und 'Hebräer.' Zu Apg 9,29 und 6,1" *BZ* (New Series) 23/1 (1979): 87-92.

719 Petersen, T. C. "An Early Coptic Manuscript of Acts: An Unrevised Version of the Ancient So-Called Western Text," *CBQ* 26/2 (1964): 225-41 [*see also* 367, 576, 908, 978].

720 Petofi, J. S. "La struttura della comunicazione in *Atti 20,17-38*," *RB* 29/3-4 (1981): 359-78.

721 Philonenki, M. "Le Décret apostolique et les interdits alimentaires du Coran," *RHPR* 47/2 (1967): 165-72.

722 Pierce, Flora M. "Glossolalia," *JRPR* 4 (1981): 168-78 [*see also* 001, 011, 012, 025, 201, 230, 239, 247, 266, 279, 322, 346, 437, 483, 552, 665, 808, 932, 973, 975].

723 Pierce, J. A. "The Twelve as Apostolic Overseers," *BibTo* 18 (1980): 72-76 [*see also* 212, 220, 345].

724 des Places, Édouard. "Actes 17,25" *Bib* 46 (1965): 219-22.

725 _____. "Actes 17,27" *Bib* 48/1 (1967): 1-6 [*see also* 017, 020, 086, 091, 132, 276, 394, 509, 604, 635, 680, 852, 980].

726 _____. "Actes 17,30-31" *Bib* 52/4 (1971): 526-34.

727 _____. "Ipsius enim et genus sumus (Act 17,28)" *Bib* 43/3 (1962): 388-95.

728 _____. "De oratione S. Pauli ad Areopagum (Apg 17,16-31)" *PIB* (1964): 5-47 [*see also* 091, 098, 132, 197, 231, 286, 394, 509, 518, 577, 635, 725, 730, 852].

729 _____. "Quasi superstitiosiores (Acta 17,22)," *AnBib* 17-18/2 (1963): 183-91.

730 _____. "Des temples faits de main d'homme (Actes des Apôtres, 17,24)" *Bib* 42/2 (1961): 217-23 [*see also* 091, 098, 132, 197, 231, 286, 394, 509, 518, 577, 635, 725, 728, 852].

731 Plassart, A. "L'inscription de Delphes mentionnant le procounsul Gallion (Act 18,12-17)," *RÉG* 80 (1967): 165-72 [*see also* 361].

732 Plevnik, Joseph. "The Eleven and Those with Them According to Luke," *CBQ* 40 (1978): 205-11.

733 Plümacher, E. "Acta-Forschung 1974-1982," *TR* 48/1 (1983): 1-56.

734 _____. "Wirklichkeitserfahrung und Geschichtesschreibung bei Lukas. Erwägungen zu den Wir-Stücken der Apostelgeschichte," *ZNW* 58/1-2 (1977): 2-22 [*see also* 004, 005, 118, 392, 501, 669].

735 Pokorný, P. "Die Romfahrt des Paulus und der antike Roman," *ZNW* 64/3-4 (1973): 233-44 [*see also* 323, 472, 564, 598, 694, 741, 784, 825, 869, 941, 965].

736 Polhill, J. B. "The Hellenist Breakthrough: Acts 6-12," *REx* 71/4: 475-86 [*see also* 254, 397, 526, 703, 728, 958].

737 Pontet, M. "Pentecôte et charité fraternelle," *Chr* 9/35 (1962): 340-54 [*see also* 006, 042, 064, 076, 078, 084, 100, 126, 128, 148, 189, 195, 196, 277, 309, 312, 315, 319, 320, 322, 327, 371, 372, 387, 403, 439, 459, 462, 475, 482, 519, 522, 528, 532, 541, 549, 574, 586, 590, 609, 611, 614, 623, 632, 643, 692, 699, 709, 755, 759, 772, 783, 784, 808, 817, 830, 864, 867, 872, 891, 894, 898, 900, 913, 917, 919, 934, 939, 944, 960, 964, 974].

738 Poque, Suzanne. "Une lecture d'Actes: 11,27-12,25," *ETR* 55/2 (1980): 265-78.

739 de la Potterie, I. "Les deux noms de Jérusalem dans Apôtres," *Bib* 63/2 (1982): 153-87 [*see also* 035, 100, 148, 167, 178, 232, 323, 372, 503, 504, 564, 609, 661, 760, 777, 784, 812, 850, 854, 869, 870, 890, 895, 941, 971, 984, 987].

740 _____. "Gesu il capo che conduce alla vita (At 3,15)," *PSV* 5 (1982): 107-26.

741 Prete, B. "L'arrivo di Paolo a Roma e il suo significato secondo *Atti* 28,16-31," *RBib* 31/2 (1983): 147-87 [*see also* 323, 472, 564, 598, 694, 735, 784, 825, 869, 941, 965].

742 _____. "Il somario di *Atti* 1,13-14 e suo aporto per la conoscenza della Chiesa delle origini," *SacD* 18/69-70 (1973): 65-125.

743 _____. "Valore dell'espressione," *BibO* 13/3 (1971): 119-33.

744 Prigent, P. "Un nouveau texte des Actes: Le Papyrus Bodmer XVII, p 74," *RHPR* 42/2-3 (1962): 169-74.

745 Pummer, Reinhard. "The Samaritan Pentateuch and the New Testament," *NTS* 22/4 (1975-1976): 441-43 [*see also* 766].

746 Quinn, Jerome D. "The Last Volume of Luke: The Relation of Luke-Acts to the Pastoral Epistles," *PRS* 5 (1978): 62-75.

747 _____. "Seven Times He Wore Chains (1 Clem 5,6)," *JBL* 97 (1978): 574-76.

748 Quispel, G. "The Discussion of Judaic Christianity," *VC* 22 (1968): 81-93.

749 Radl, W. "Das 'Apostelkonzil' und seine Nachgeschichte, dargestellt am Weg des Brnabas," *TQ* 162/1 (1982): 45-61 [*see also* 245, 267, 282, 288, 330, 347, 638, 653, 895].

750 _____. "Befreiung aus dem Gefängnis. Die Darstellung eines biblischen Grundthemas in Apg 12," *BZ* 27/1 (1983): 81-96.

751 _____. "Paulus traditus. Jesus und sein Missionar im lukanischen Doppelwerk," *EA* 50/3 (1974): 163-67.

752 Ragot, A. "D'Apollos a Hermas," *CahC* 18/71 (1971): 45-50.

753 Ramaroson, L. "Contre les temples faits du mains d'hommes (Acts 7,48; 17,24)" *RPH* 43 (1969): 217-38.

754 Rasco, E. "Beauté et exigences de la communion ecclésiale (Ac 2; 4; 5)" *AS* (New Series) 23 (1970): 6-23.

755 _____. "Dans l'attente de l'Espirit, le choix d'un nouvel apôtre (Ac 1)" *AS* (New Series) 29 (1970): 6-18 [*see also* 006, 042, 064, 076, 078, 084, 100, 126, 128, 148, 189, 195, 196, 277, 309, 312, 315, 319, 320, 322, 327, 371, 372, 387, 403, 439, 459, 462, 475, 482, 519, 522, 528, 532, 541, 549, 574, 586, 590, 609, 611, 614, 623, 632, 643, 692, 699, 709, 737, 759, 772, 783, 784, 808, 817, 830, 864, 867, 872, 891, 894, 898, 900, 913, 917, 919, 934, 939, 944, 960, 964, 974].

756 _____. "La gloire de la résurrection et ses fruits, Act 2,14,22-28; 3,13-15,17-19; 5,27b-32,40b-41," *AssS* 24 (1969): 6-14 [*see also* 024, 055, 058, 077, 142, 168, 223, 334, 343, 363, 386, 458, 462, 506, 508, 609, 675, 678, 683, 763, 803, 832, 862, 950].

757 Ravanelli, V. "La testimonianza di Stefano su Gesù Cristo," *SBFLA* 24 (1974): 121-41 [*see also* 016, 769, 820, 867].

758 Ravarotto, E. "De Hierosolymitano Concilio (Act. Cap. 15)" *Anton* 37/2 (1962): 185-218 [*see also* 029, 178, 234, 245, 251, 281, 408, 414, 461, 617, 662, 711, 713, 847, 857].

759 Rayan, A. "The Growth of the Church in the Acts," *Bhash* 4/2 (1978): 98-116 [*see also* 006, 042, 064, 076, 078, 084, 100, 126, 128, 148, 189, 195, 196, 277, 309, 312, 315, 319, 320, 322, 327, 371, 372, 387, 403, 439, 459, 462, 475, 482, 519, 522, 528, 532, 541, 549, 574, 586, 590, 609, 611, 614, 623, 632, 643, 692, 699, 709, 737, 755, 772, 783, 784, 808, 817, 830, 864, 867, 872, 891, 894, 898, 900, 913, 917, 919, 934, 939, 944, 960, 964, 974].

760 Redalie, Y. "Conversion ou liberation? Notes sur Actes 16,11-40," *BCPE* 26/7 (1974): 7-17 [*see also* 035, 100, 148, 167, 178, 232, 323, 372, 503, 504, 564, 609, 661, 739, 777, 784, 812, 850, 854, 869, 870, 890, 895, 941, 971, 984, 987].

761 Reese, B. "The Apostle Paul's Exercise of his Rights as a Roman Citizen as Recorded in the Book of Acts," *EvQ* 47/3 (1975): 138-45.

762 Renehan, R. "Acts 17:28," *GRBS* 20/4 (1979): 347-53.

763 Rengstorf, K. H. "Die Zuwahl des Matthias (Apg 1,15 ff.)" *ST* 15/1 (1961): 35-67 [*see also* 173, 176, 332, 336, 559, 567, 654, 687].

764 Reyero, S. " 'Durum est tibi contra stimulum calcitrare.' Hechos de los Apóstoles, 26, 14," *Stud* 10/2 (1970): 367-78.

765 Richard, E. "Acts 6:1-8:4: The Author's Method of Composition," *CuTM* 6 (1979): 374.

766 _____. "Acts 7: An Investigation of the Samaritan Evidence," *CBQ* 39/2 (1977): 190-208 [*see also* 745].

767 _____. "The Creative Use of Amos by the Author of Acts," *NT* 24/1 (1982): 37-53.

768 _____. "The Old Testament in Acts: Wilcox's Semitisms in Retrospect," *CBQ* 42/3 (1980): 330-41 [*see also* 505, 888].

769 _____. "The Polemical Character of the Joseph Episode in Acts 7," *JBL* 98/2 (1979): 255-67 [*see also* 016, 026, 059, 063, 075, 122, 129, 180, 188, 311, 323, 327, 397, 464, 486, 487, 504, 526, 571, 690, 707, 716, 717, 757, 820, 837, 847, 848, 849, 881, 886, 912, 928, 950, 958].

770 Richardson, W. "A Motif of Greek Philosophy in Luke-Acts," *SEv* 2 (1963): 628-34.

771 Riecke, Bo. "Apostlagarningarnas teologi (Die Thiolohie der Apg)(schwed)," *SEÅ* 36 (1960): 1-12.

772 Riedl, J. "Der Heilige Geist wird euch in alle Wahrheit einführen (Joh 16,13)" *BiLi* 44 (1971): 89-94 [*see also* 006, 042, 064, 076, 078, 084, 100, 126, 128, 148, 189, 195, 196, 277, 309, 312, 315, 319, 320, 322, 327, 371, 372, 387, 403, 439, 459, 462, 475, 482, 519, 522, 528, 532, 541, 549, 574, 586, 590, 609, 611, 614, 623, 632, 643, 692, 699, 709, 737, 755, 759, 783, 784, 808, 817, 830, 864, 867, 872, 891, 894, 898, 900, 913, 917, 919, 934, 939, 944, 960, 964, 974].

773 _____. "Österliches Christentum: 'Wir können unmöglich von dem schweigen, was wir gesehen und gehört haben,' " *BiLi* 39 (1966): 72-84.

774 _____. "Sabed que Dios envía su salud a los gentiles (Hch 28,28)" *RBib* 27 (1965): 153-55, 162 [*see also* 144, 363, 382, 427, 449, 524, 538, 683, 701, 782, 935, 944, 969].

775 Riekert, S. J. "Stilistiese moontlikhede en die werklike of vermeende teksprobleme in die proloog van Handelinge," *NGTT* 22/3 (1981): 179-87 [*see also* 093, 364].

776 Riesenfeld, Harald. "The Text of Acts 10:36," *TI* (1979): 191-94.

777 Rinaldi, Giovanni. "Comunità cristiane nell'età Apostolica," *BibO* 12/1 (1970): 3-10 [*see also* 003, 021, 133, 296, 308, 355, 445, 512, 551, 569, 632, 703, 801, 810, 897, 927, 928].

778 _____. "Giacomo, Paolo e i Giudei (Atti 21, 17-26)" *RBib* 14/4 (1966): 407-23.

779 _____. "La lingua et le lingue," *BibO* 4/3 (1962): 85-94.

780 _____. "Lógos in Atti 10,36" *BibO* 12/4-5 (1970): 223-25 [*see also* 484].

781 _____. "Nota: Dike in Atti 28,4," *BibO* 24/133 (1982): 186.

782 _____. "Stefano," *BibO* 6/4-5 (1964): 153-62 [*see also* 144, 363, 382, 427, 449, 524, 538, 683, 701, 774, 935, 944, 969].

783 Rius-Camps, J. "L'aparicio/desaparicio des 'nosaltres' en el libre dels Fets: un simple procediment teologico-literari?" *RCT* 6/1 (1981): 33-75 [*see also* 006, 042, 064, 076, 078, 084, 100, 126, 128, 148, 189, 195, 196, 277, 309, 312, 315, 319, 320, 322, 327, 371, 372, 387, 403, 439, 459, 462, 475, 482, 519, 522, 528, 532, 541, 549, 574, 586, 590, 609, 611, 614, 623, 632, 643, 692, 699, 709, 737, 755, 759, 772, 784, 808, 817, 830, 864, 867, 872, 891, 894, 898, 900, 913, 917, 919, 934, 939, 944, 960, 964, 974].

784 _____. "Questions sobre la doble obra lucana. I. La darrera pujada du Pau a Jerusalem: 'Desviació' del camí cap a Roma," *RCT* 5/1 (1980): 1-94 [*see also* 035, 100, 148, 167, 178, 232, 323, 372, 503, 504, 564, 609, 661, 739, 760, 777, 812, 850, 854, 869, 870, 890, 895, 941, 971, 984, 987].

785 _____. "Questions sobre la doble obra lucana. II Qui és Joan, l'anomenat 'Marc'?" *RCT* 5/2 (1980): 297-329 [*see also* 050, 107, 162, 176, 181, 219, 245, 250, 252, 328, 414, 498, 640, 645, 658, 672, 711, 787, 815, 942, 964, 965].

786 Rivera, Luis Fernando. "De Christo a la Iglesia," *RBib* 31/2 (1969): 97-105.

787 _____. "El nacimiento de la Iglesia," *RBib* 31 (1969): 35-45 [*see also* 038, 187, 278, 425, 537, 654, 963, 970].

788 Robbins, V. K. "By Land and by Sea: The We-Passages and Ancient Sea Voyages," *PRS* 5 (1978): 215-42 [*see also* 028 182, 280, 283, 366, 734, 783, 789].

789 _____. "The 'We' Passages in Acts and Ancient Voyages," *BiR* 20 (1975): 1-18 [*see also* 060, 237, 358, 367, 377, 378, 460, 490, 511, 537, 578, 698, 788, 827, 862, 896, 908, 910, 914, 926, 955, 970, 977].

790 Robeck, C. "The Gift of Prophecy in Acts and Paul, Part I," *SBT* 5 (1975): 15-38.

791 Roberts, J. H. "Ekklēsia in Acts—Linguistic and Theology: A Venture in Methodology," *Neo* 7 (1973): 73-93.

792 _____. "*Pais Theou* and *Ho Huios tou Theou* in Acts 1-13," *OT* (1966): 239-63 [*see also* 010, 016, 374, 423, 466, 482, 488, 502, 533, 555, 581, 626, 629, 677, 863, 900, 953].

793 Robinson, J. A. T. "Ascendancy," *ANQ* 5/2 (1964): 5-9 [*see also* 055, 154, 175, 207, 210, 269, 274, 335, 368, 369, 462, 506, 508, 531, 536, 539, 540, 612, 614, 827, 959, 977].

794 Robinson, M. A. "Spermologos: Did Paul Preach from Jesus' Parables?" *Bib* 56/2 (1975): 231-40 [*see also* 405].

795 Rodenas, Angel. "San Pablo sometido al psicoanalisis: ¿Un mundo paranoico?" *CuBi* 34 (1977): 167-77 [*see also* 044, 089, 180, 252, 288, 645, 653, 661, 708, 815, 877, 893, 942, 980].

796 Rolland, P. "L'organisation du Livre des Actes et de l'ensemble de l'oeuvre de Luc," *Bib* 65/1 (1984): 81-86.

797 Rouge, J. "Actes 27,1-10," *VC* 14/4 (1960): 193-203.

798 Royse, J. R. "The Ethiopic Support for Codex Vaticanus in Acts," *ZNW* 71/3-4 (1980): 258-62.

799 Rudolph, K. "Simon—Magus oder Gnosticus? Zur Stand der Debatte," *TR* 42/4 (1977): 279-359 [*see also* 008, 037, 048, 174, 365, 670, 868].

800 Russell, E. A. "They Believed Philip Preaching (Acts 8:12)" *IBS* 1 (1979): 169-76 [*see also* 037, 063, 109, 174, 208, 270, 602, 603, 681, 690].

801 Russo, A. "Gli Atti degli Apostoli e la fede della primitiva comunità guiden-cristiana," *RLSE* 2 (1970): 282-95 [*see also* 003, 021, 133, 296, 308, 355, 445, 512, 551, 569, 632, 703, 777, 810, 897, 927, 928].

802 Rutledge, Arthur B. "Evangelistic Methods in Acts," *SWJT* 17/1 (1974): 35-47 [*see also* 244, 407].

803 Ryan, W. F. J. "The church as the Servant of God in Acts," *Sc* 15/32 (1963): 110-15 [*see also* 024, 055, 058, 077, 142, 168, 223, 334, 343, 363, 386, 458, 462, 506, 508, 609, 675, 678, 683, 756, 763, 832, 862, 950].

804 Sabugal, S. "La conversion de S. Pablo en Damasco: ciudad de Siria o region de Qumran?" *Aug* 15/5 (1975): 213-24 [*see also* 389, 457, 516, 607, 882].

805 _____. "La Mencion neotestamentaria de Damasco (Gal 1,17; 2 Cor 11,32; Act 9,2-3.8.10 par 19,22,27 par) ¿ciudad de Siria o region de Qumran?" *BETL* 45 (1978): 403-13 [*see also* 038, 146, 233, 255, 262, 420, 513, 597, 804, 947].

806 Sahagian, S. "Tonalités de la parole. 4—Temps de l'Église— Actes 2/1-13," *ETR* 58/3 (1983): 359-67 [*see also* 001, 043, 076, 077, 078, 088, 101, 110, 121, 126, 154, 178, 190, 221, 239, 240, 242, 300, 340, 370, 465, 493, 512, 528, 541, 577, 590, 611, 613, 624, 644, 665, 687, 692, 737, 787, 808, 812, 813, 817, 862, 888, 900, 902, 930, 939, 960, 964, 975].

807 Sahlin, H. "Emendationsvorschläge zum griechischen Text des Neuen Testaments II," *NT* 24/2 (1982): 180-89.

808 Salas, A. "Estaban 'todos' reunidos (Hch 2,1). Precisiones críticas sobre los 'testigos' de Pentecostés," *Salmanticensis* 28/1-2 (1981): 299-314 [*see also* 006, 042, 064, 076, 078, 084, 100, 126, 128, 148, 189, 195, 196, 277, 309, 312, 315, 319, 320, 322, 327, 371, 372, 387, 403, 439, 459, 462, 475, 482, 519, 522, 528, 532, 541, 549, 574, 586, 590, 609, 611, 614, 623, 632, 643, 692, 699, 709, 737, 755, 759, 772, 783, 784, 817, 830, 864, 867, 872, 891, 894, 898, 900, 913, 917, 919, 934, 939, 944, 960, 964, 974].

809 Saldarini, A. J. "Last Words and Deathbed Scenes," *JQR* 68 (1977): 28-45.

810 Salguero, J. "La comunità cristiana primitiva," *SacD* 14/54 (1969): 217-49 [*see also* 003, 021, 133, 296, 308, 355, 445, 512, 551, 569, 632, 703, 777, 801, 897, 927, 928].

811 Salvador, J. "O Querigma nos Atos dos Apóstolos," *RCB* 9/3-4 (1972): 105-34.

812 Samain, E. "A Igreja, uma Communidade Libertadora e Criadora? Uma exegese de Atos 2,1-13," *REB* 35 (1975): 326-62 [*see also* 035, 100, 148, 167, 178, 232, 323, 372, 503, 504, 564, 609, 661, 739, 760, 777, 784, 850, 854, 869, 870, 890, 895, 941, 971, 984, 987].

813 _____. "Le récit de la Pentecôte, Act 2,1-13," *FT* N.S. (1971): 227-56 [*see also* 001, 043, 076, 077, 078, 088, 101, 110, 121, 126, 154, 178, 190, 221, 239, 240, 242, 300, 340, 370, 465, 493, 512, 528, 541, 577, 590, 611, 613, 624, 644, 665, 687, 692, 737, 787, 806, 808, 812, 817, 862, 888, 900, 902, 930, 939, 960, 964, 975].

814 Sand, A. "Überlegungen zur gegenwartigen Diskussion über den 'Frühkatholizismus' " *Cath* 33 (1979): 49-62.

815 Sanders, J. N. "Peter and Paul in Acts," *NTS* 3 (1955-1956): 133ff [*see also* 044, 089, 180, 252, 288, 645, 653, 661, 708, 795, 877, 893, 942, 980].

816 Saum, F. "Er lebte . . . von seinem eigenen Einkommen (Apg 28,30)," *BZ* 20/2 (1976): 226-29.

817 Sauvagnat, B. "Se repentir, être baptisé, recevoir L'Esprit, Actes 2,37ss," *FS* 80 (1981): 77-89 [*see also* 152, 196, 270, 315, 324, 448, 488, 603, 673, 699, 907, 974].

818 Saydon, P. P. "The Site of St. Paul's Shipwreck," *MT* 14/1-2 (1962): 58-61 [*see also* 605, 618, 669].

819 Schalit, A. "Zu AG 25,9," *ASTI* 6 (1968): 106-13 [*see also* 209, 679].

820 Scharlemann, M. H. "Acts 7:2-53. Stephen's Speech: A Lucan Creation?" *CJ* 4/2 (1978): 52-57 [*see also* 016, 757, 867].

821 Schenke, L. "Die Apostelgeschichte," *ZZ* 23 (1969): 458-63.

822 _____. "Glaube im lukanischen Doppelwerk," *BTSt* 7 (1982): 69-92.

823 _____. "Die Kontrastformel Apg 4,10b," *BZ* 26/1 (1982): 1-20.

824 Schepens, G. "Lucas, hellenisme en christendom. Beschouwingen over 'De Handelingen der Apostelen,' " *Col* 31/1 (1984): 31-55.

825 Schierling, S. P. and M. J. Schierling. "The Influence of the Ancient Romances on Acts of the Apostles," *CB* 54/6 (1978): 81-88 [*see also* 323, 472, 564, 598, 694, 735, 741, 784, 869, 941, 965].

826 Schierse, F. J. "Geschichte und Geschichten. Hermeneutische Überlegungen zur Apostelgeschichte," *BiKi* 31/2 (1976): 34-38.

827 Schille, G. "Die Himmelfahrt," *ZNW* 57/3-4 (1966): 183-99 [*see also* 055, 154, 175, 207, 210, 269, 274, 335, 368, 369, 462, 506, 508, 531, 536, 539, 540, 612, 614, 793, 959, 977].

828 _____. "Die Leistung des Lukas in der Apostelgeschichte," *TVer* 7 (1976): 91-106.

829 Schlemmer, A. "L'Église du livre des Actes est-elle normative," *RevR* 7/27 (1956): 73-79.

830 Schmidt, Karl. "Das Pneuma Hagion als Person und als Charisma," *EJ* 13 (1965): 187-231 [*see also* 006, 042, 064, 076, 078, 084, 100, 126, 128, 148, 189, 195, 196, 277, 309, 312, 315, 319, 320, 322, 327, 371, 372, 387, 403, 439, 459, 462, 475, 482, 519, 522, 528, 532, 541, 549, 574, 586, 590, 609, 611, 614, 623, 632, 643, 692, 699, 709, 737, 755, 759, 772, 783, 784, 808, 817, 864, 867, 872, 891, 894, 898, 900, 913, 917, 919, 934, 939, 944, 960, 964, 974].

831 Schmithals, W. "Die Berichte der Apostelgeschichte über die Bekehrung des Paulus und die 'Tendenz' des Lukas," *TVia* 14 (1977): 145-65.

832 Schmitt, A. "Ps 16,8-11 als Zeugnis der Auferstehung in der Apg," *BZ* 17 /2 (1973): 229-48 [*see also* 024, 055, 058, 077, 142, 168, 223, 334, 343, 363, 386, 458, 462, 506, 508, 609, 675, 678, 683, 756, 763, 803, 862, 950].

833 Schmitt, J. "L'autorité de la Tradition aux temps apostoliques," *RScR* 53 (1979): 209-19,

834 _____. "Les discours missionnaires des Actes et l'histoire des traditions prépauliniennes," *RSR* 69/2 (1981): 165-80.

835 Schneider, Gerhard. "Apostelgeschichte und Kirchengeschichte," *Com* 8/6 (1979): 481-87 [*see also* 194, 430, 479, 947].

836 _____. "Die Apostelgeschichte. II. Teil: Kommentar zu Kap 9,1-28,31," *NT* 5/2 (1982): 5-440.

837 _____. "Stephanus, die Hellenisten und Samaria," *BETL* 48 (1979): 215-40 [*see also* 159, 171].

838 Schoonheim, P. L. "De centurio Cornelius," *NTT* 18/6 (1964): 453-75 [*see also* 108, 129, 250, 360, 542, 573, 587, 658, 688, 873].

839 Schubert, Paul. "The Final Cycle of Speeches in the Book of Acts," *JBL* 87/1 (1968): 1-16 [*see also* 070, 096, 115, 193, 199, 326, 497, 554, 647, 846, 867, 921, 968].

840 Schulz, Siegfried. "Die Mitte der Schrift: der Fruhkatholizismus im NT," *TZ* 34 (1978): 113s.

841 Schwank, B. " 'Setz über nach Mazedonien und hilf uns!' Reisenotizen zu Apg 16,9-17,5" *EA* 39/5 (1963): 399-416 [*see also* 047, 069, 151, 155, 156, 163, 166, 280, 329, 476, 615, 949, 984].

842 _____. " 'Und so kamen wir nach Rom (Apg 28,14). ' Reisenotizen zu den letzten beiden Kapiteln der Apostelgeschichte," *EA* 36/3 (1960): 169-93.

843 _____. " 'Wir umsegelten Kreta bei Salmone.' Reisebericht zu Apg 27,7-12," *EA* 48/1 (1972): 16-25.

844 Schwartz, D. R. "Non-Joining Sympathizers (Acts 5,13-14)," *Bib* 64/4 (1983): 550-55 [*see also* 172, 611, 962].

845 Scobie, C. H. H. "The Origins and Development of Samaritan Christianity," *NTS* 19 (1972-1973): 390-414.

846 _____. "The Use of Source Material in the Speeches of Acts III and VII," *NTS* 25/4 (1978-1979): 339-421 [*see also* 070, 096, 115, 193, 199, 326, 497, 554, 647, 839, 867, 921, 968].

847 Scott, J. J., Jr. "Parties in the Church of Jerusalem as Seen in the Book of Acts," *JETS* 18/4 (1975): 217-27 [*see also* 029, 178, 234, 245, 251, 281, 408, 414, 461, 617, 662, 711, 713, 758, 857].

848 _____. "Stephen's Defense and the World Mission of the People of God," *JETS* 21/2 (1978): 131-41 [*see also* 136, 149, 200, 295, 359, 518, 522, 538, 558, 591, 646, 683, 703, 905, 961].

849 _____. "Stephen's Speech: A Possible Model for Luke's Historical Method?" *JETS* 17/2 (1974): 91-97.

850 Seguy, Jean. "Anabaptisme pacifique, houtterianisme et communaute Jerusalemité Zur Wirkgeschichte der Apg," *LVie* 30/153 (1981): 150-66 [*see also* 035, 100, 148, 167, 178, 232, 323, 372, 503, 504, 564, 609, 661, 739, 760, 777, 784, 812, 854, 869, 870, 890, 895, 941, 971, 984, 987].

851 Sena, P. J. "The Acts of the Apostles," *BibTo* 95 (1978): 1546-52.

852 Shields, B. E. "The Areopagus Sermon and Romans 1:10ff: A Study in Creation Theology," *RQ* 20/1 (1977): 23-40 [*see also* 017, 020, 086, 091, 132, 276, 394, 509, 604, 635, 680, 725, 980].

853 Sieben, Hermann-Joseph. "Zur Entwicklung der Konzilsidee X: Die Konzilsidee des Lukas," *TP* 50/4 (1975): 481-503.

854 Siegel, J. P. "The Alexandrians in Jerusalem and Their Torah Scroll with Gold Tetragrammata," *IEJ* 22/1 (1972): 39-43 [*see also* 035, 100, 148, 167, 178, 232, 323, 372, 503, 504, 564, 609, 661, 739, 760, 777, 784, 812, 850, 869, 870, 890, 895, 941, 971, 984, 987].

855 Silva, Rafael. "Eran, pues, de oficio, fabricantes de tiendas σκηνοποιοί (Act 18,3)" *EB* 24/1-2 (1965): 123-34.

856 Silvola, Kalevi. "Apostolien tekojen lahetyspuheiden engelma (Das Problem der Missionsreden in Apg)," *TA* 79/6 (1974): 547-60.

857 Simon, M. "The Apostolic Decree and its Setting in the Ancient Church," *BJRL* 52/2 (1970): 437-60 [*see also* 029, 178, 234, 245, 251, 281, 408, 414, 461, 617, 662, 711, 713, 758, 847].

858 _____. "De l'observance rituelle à l'ascèse: recherches sur le Décret Apostolique," *RHR* 193/1 27-104.

859 _____. "La prière non religieuse chez Luc," *FV* 74 (1975): 8-22.

860 Sinnemaki, Maunu. "Pelastus ja rauhanvaltakunta. Raamatullinen nakokulma," *TA* 82/6 (1977): 527-45.

861 Sisti, Adalberto. "Il nome di Gesu negli Atti degli Apostoli," *Anton* 55/4 (1980): 675-94.

862 Sleeper, C. F. "Pentecost and Resurrection," *JBL* 84/4 (1965): 389-99 [*see also* 001, 043, 076, 077, 078, 088, 101, 110, 121, 126, 154, 178, 190, 221, 239, 240, 242, 300, 340, 370, 465, 493, 512, 528, 541, 577, 590, 611, 613, 624, 644, 665, 687, 692, 737, 787, 806, 808, 812, 813, 817, 888, 900, 902, 930, 939, 960, 964, 975].

863 Smalley, S. S. "The Christology of Acts," *ET* 73/12 (1962): 358-62 [*see also* 010, 016, 374, 423, 466, 482, 488, 502, 533, 555, 581, 626, 629, 677, 792, 900, 953].

864 _____. "Spirit, Kingdom and Prayer in Luke-Acts," *NT* 15 (1973): 59-71 [*see also* 006, 042, 064, 076, 078, 084, 100, 126, 128, 148, 189, 195, 196, 277, 309, 312, 315, 319, 320, 322, 327, 371, 372, 387, 403, 439, 459, 462, 475, 482, 519, 522, 528, 532, 541, 549, 574, 586, 590, 609, 611, 614, 623, 632, 643, 692, 699, 709, 737, 755, 759, 772, 783, 784, 808, 817, 830, 867, 872, 891, 894, 898, 900, 913, 917, 919, 934, 939, 944, 960, 964, 974].

865 Smith, R. H. "The Theology of Acts," *CTM* 42/8 (1971): 527-35 [*see also* 196, 401, 817, 906].

866 Snydere, H. A. "The Community of the King," *CTJ* 13 (1978): 246-50.

867 Soffritti, O. "Stefano, testimone del Signore," *RBib* 10/2 (1962): 182-88 [*see also* 006, 042, 064, 076, 078, 084, 100, 126, 128, 148, 189, 195, 196, 277, 309, 312, 315, 319, 320, 322, 327, 371, 372, 387, 403, 439, 459, 462, 475, 482, 519, 522, 528, 532, 541, 549, 574, 586, 590, 609, 611, 614, 623, 632, 643, 692, 699, 709, 737, 755, 759, 772, 783, 784, 808, 817, 830, 864, 872, 891, 894, 898, 900, 913, 917, 919, 934, 939, 944, 960, 964, 974].

868 Sokolowski, F. "A New Testimony on the Cult of Artemis of Ephesus," *HTR* 58/4 (1965): 427-31 [*see also* 088, 390, 436, 451, 467, 674, 700, 924].

869 Songer, H. S. "Paul's Mission to Jerusalem: Acts 20-28," *REx* 71/4 (1974): 499-510 [*see also* 035, 100, 148, 167, 178, 232, 323, 372, 503, 504, 564, 609, 661, 739, 760, 777, 784, 812, 850, 854, 870, 890, 895, 941, 971, 984, 987].

870 Speyer, W. "Die Zeugungskraft des himmlischen Feuers in (griechischromischer) Antike und Urchristentum (der Blitzglaube, auch das pyr phronimon/noeron; Keraunos/phallos; Pfingstbericht; Taufe Jesu...)," *AntAb* 24 (1978): 57-78 [*see also* 035, 100, 148, 167, 178, 232, 323, 372, 503, 504, 564, 609, 661, 739, 760, 777, 784, 812, 850, 854, 869, 890, 895, 941, 971, 984, 987].

871 Spicq, C. "Ce que signifie le titre de chrétien," *ST* 15/1 (1961): 68-78.

872 da Spongano, B. "La concezione teologica della predicazione nel libro degli 'Atti,' " *RBib* 21/2 (1973): 147-64 [*see also* 006, 042, 064, 076, 078, 084, 100, 126, 128, 148, 189, 195, 196, 277, 309, 312, 315, 319, 320, 322, 327, 371, 372, 387, 403, 439, 459, 462, 475, 482, 519, 522, 528, 532, 541, 549, 574, 586, 590, 609, 611, 614, 623, 632, 643, 692, 699, 709, 737, 755, 759, 772, 783, 784, 808, 817, 830, 864, 867, 891, 894, 898, 900, 913, 917, 919, 934, 939, 944, 960, 964, 974].

873 Squillaci, D. "La conversione del centurio Cornelio," *PC* 39 (1960): 1265-69 [*see also* 108, 129, 250, 360, 542, 573, 587, 658, 688, 838].

874 _____. "La conversione dell'Etiope," *PC* 39/22 (1960): 1197-1201 [*see also* 206, 213, 401, 457, 563, 621, 670, 691, 873, 906].

875 _____. "La frazione del pane," *PC* 39/17 (1960): 913-17.

876 _____. "Nel XIX Centenario Paolino—II primo Concilio e San Paolo," *PC* 40 (August 1-15, 1961): 829-34.

877 _____. "San Paolo in Efeso (Atti c. 19)," *PC* 40 (November 1, 1961): 1137-44 [*see also* 044, 089, 180, 252, 288, 645, 653, 661, 708, 795, 815, 893, 942, 980].

878 Stagg, F. "A Teaching Outline for Acts," *REx* 71 (1974): 533-36.

879 _____. "The Unhindered Gospel," *REx* 71/4 (1974): 451-62.

880 Stanley, D. M. "Die Predigt der Urkirche und ihr traditionelles Schema," *Conc* 2/10 (1966): 787-93.

881 Stanton, Graham. "Stephen in Lucan Perspective," *StB* 3 (1980): 345-60 [*see also* 016, 026, 059, 063, 075, 122, 129, 180, 188, 311, 323, 327, 397, 464, 486, 487, 504, 526, 571, 690, 707, 716, 717, 757, 769, 820, 837, 847, 848, 849, 886, 912, 928, 950, 958].

882 Steck, O. H. "Formgeschichtliche Bemerkungen zur Darstellung des Damaskusgeschehens in der Apostelgeschichte," *ZNW* 67/1-2 (1976): 20-28 [*see also* 389, 457, 516, 607, 804].

883 Stein, R. H. "The Relationship of Galatians 2:1-10 and Acts 15:1-35: Two Neglected Arguments," *JETS* 17 (n.d.): 239-42.

884 Steinmetz, F. J. "Sie sahen die Wunder, die er tat," *GeL* 46 (1973): 99-114.

885 Stemberger, G. "Stammt das synodale Element der Kirche aus der Synogage?" *AHC* 8/1-2 (1976): 1-14.

886 _____. "Die Stephanusrede (Apg 7) und die judische Tradition," *SNTU* 1 (1976): 154-74 [*see also* 016, 026, 059, 063, 075, 122, 129, 180, 188, 311, 323, 327, 397, 464, 486, 487, 504, 526, 571, 690, 707, 716, 717, 757, 769, 820, 837, 847, 848, 849, 881, 912, 928, 950, 958].

887 van Stempvoort, P. A. "Het leip tegen de vijtigste dag. De betekenis van Hand. 2:1," *HB* 21/5 (1962): 97-103.

888 Stenger, Werner. "Beobachtungen zur sogenannten Völkerliste des Pfingstwunders (Apg 2,7-11)" *K* 21/2-3 (1979): 206-14 [*see also* 001, 043, 076, 077, 078, 088, 101, 110, 121, 126, 154, 178, 190, 221, 239, 240, 242, 300, 340, 370, 465, 493, 512, 528, 541, 577, 590, 611, 613, 624, 644, 665, 687, 692, 737, 787, 806, 808, 812, 813, 817, 862, 900, 902, 930, 939, 960, 964, 975].

889 Stevenson, D. E. "Preaching From the Book of Acts," *REx 71* (1974): 511-19.

890 Stöger, A. "Jerusalem—Rom. Neue Kommentare zur Apostelgeschichte," *BiLi* 55/2 (1982): 102-105 [*see also* 035, 100, 148, 167, 178, 232, 323, 372, 503, 504, 564, 609, 661, 739, 760, 777, 784, 812, 850, 854, 869, 870, 895, 941, 971, 984, 987].

891 Stoyannos, V. P. " 'Pneuma Pythōnia' (Pr. 16,16). Hē syn-
antēsē tou archegonou christianismou me tē mantikē," *DBM*
9/2 (1980): 99-114 [*see also* 006, 042, 064, 076, 078, 084,
100, 126, 128, 148, 189, 195, 196, 277, 309, 312, 315, 319,
320, 322, 327, 371, 372, 387, 403, 439, 459, 462, 475, 482,
519, 522, 528, 532, 541, 549, 574, 586, 590, 609, 611, 614,
623, 632, 643, 692, 699, 709, 737, 755, 759, 772, 783, 784,
808, 817, 830, 864, 867, 872, 894, 898, 900, 913, 917, 919,
934, 939, 944, 960, 964, 974].

892 Stowers, S. "The Synagogue in the Theology of Acts," *RQ* 17/
3 (1974): 129-43 [*see also* 001, 672, 705].

893 van Straelen, H. "Paulus und die anonymen Christen," *TPQ* 114/
4 (1966): 332-39 [*see also* 044, 089, 180, 252, 288, 645, 653,
661, 708, 795, 815, 877, 942, 980].

894 Stravinskas, P. M. J. "The Role of the Spirit in Acts 1 and 2,"
BibTo 18 (1980): 263-68 [*see also* 006, 042, 064, 076, 078,
084, 100, 126, 128, 148, 189, 195, 196, 277, 309, 312, 315,
319, 320, 322, 327, 371, 372, 387, 403, 439, 459, 462, 475,
482, 519, 522, 528, 532, 541, 549, 574, 586, 590, 609, 611,
614, 623, 632, 643, 692, 699, 709, 737, 755, 759, 772, 783,
784, 808, 817, 830, 864, 867, 872, 891, 898, 900, 913, 917,
919, 934, 939, 944, 960, 964, 974].

895 Strecker, G. "Die sogenannte zweite Jerusalemreise des Paulus," *ZNW* 53/1-2 (1962): 67-77 [*see also* 106, 129, 184, 201,
435, 454, 498, 527, 554, 601, 701].

896 Strobel, A. "Armenpfleger 'um des Friedens willen,' " *ZNW* 63/
3-4 (1972): 271-76 [*see also* 060, 237, 358, 367, 377, 378,
460, 490, 511, 537, 578, 698, 789, 827, 862, 908, 910, 914,
926, 955, 970, 977].

897 Sudbrack, Josef. "Die Schar der Gläubigen war ein Herz und eine
Seele (Apg 4,32)," *GeL* 38/3 (1965): 161-68 [*see also* 003,
021, 133, 296, 308, 355, 445, 512, 551, 569, 632, 703, 777,
801, 810, 927, 928].

898 Svéda, Sidonius. "Ich gieße meinen Geist auf alles Fleisch (Joel 3,1). Alttestamentliche Geistverheißung in lukanischer Deutung," *BiKi* 21/2 (1966): 37-41 [*see also* 006, 042, 064, 076, 078, 084, 100, 126, 128, 148, 189, 195, 196, 277, 309, 312, 315, 319, 320, 322, 327, 371, 372, 387, 403, 439, 459, 462, 475, 482, 519, 522, 528, 532, 541, 549, 574, 586, 590, 609, 611, 614, 623, 632, 643, 692, 699, 709, 737, 755, 759, 772, 783, 784, 808, 817, 830, 864, 867, 872, 891, 894, 900, 913, 917, 919, 934, 939, 944, 960, 964, 974].

899 Swain, L. "The Meaning of the Acts of the Apostles," *CRev* 51/7 (1966): 535-40.

900 _____. "Pentecost and the New Covenant," *CRev* 51/5 (1966): 369-77 [*see also* 010, 016, 374, 423, 466, 482, 488, 502, 533, 555, 581, 626, 629, 677, 792, 863, 953].

901 Synge, F. C. "Studies in Texts: Acts 13,9," *T* 63/479 (1960): 199-200.

902 Tachau, P. "Die Pfingstgeschichte nach Lukas. Exegetische Ueberlegungen zu Apg. 2,1-13," *EvE* 29 (1977): 86-102.

903 Tajra, H. W. "L'appel à César: séparation d'avec le Christianisme?" *ETR* 56/4 (1981): 593-98 [*see also* 103, 158].

904 Talbert, C. H. "An Introduction to Acts," *REx* 71/4 (1974): 437-49.

905 Ternant, P. "L'Esprit du Christ et L'intervention humaine dans l'envoi en mission en époque néotestamentaire," *NRT* 95 (1973): 367-92 [*see also* 136, 149, 200, 295, 359, 518, 522, 538, 558, 591, 646, 683, 703, 848, 961].

906 _____. "Repentez-vous et convertissez-vous (Ac 3,19)," *AssS* 21 (1963): 50-79 [*see also* 206, 213, 401, 457, 563, 621, 670, 691, 873, 874].

907 Terry, Bruce. "Baptized in One Spirit," *RQ* 21/4 (1978): 193-299 [*see also* 152, 196, 270, 315, 324, 448, 488, 603 673, 699, 817, 974].

908 Thiele, W. "Ausgewählte Biespiele zur Charakterisierung des 'westlichen' Texte der Apostelgeschichte," *ZNW* 56/1-2 (1965): 51-63 [*see also* 060, 237, 358, 367, 377, 378, 460, 490, 511, 537, 578, 698, 789, 827, 862, 896, 910, 914, 926, 955, 970, 977].

909 _____. "Eine Bermerkung zu Act 1:14," *ZNW* 53/1-2 (1962): 110-11 [*see also* 160, 162, 166, 377, 553, 695, 714].

910 Thomas, J. "Formgesetze des Begriffs-Katalogs im N.T.," *TZ* 24/1 (1968): 15-28 [*see also* 358, 472, 888].

911 Thornton, T. C. G. " 'Continuing Steadfast in Prayer'—New Light on a New Testament Phrase," *ET* 83/1 (1971): 23-24 [*see also* 911].

912 _____. "Stephen's Use of Isaiah LXVI.1," *JTS* 25/2 (1974): 432-34 [*see also* 016, 026, 059, 063, 075, 122, 129, 180, 188, 311, 323, 327, 397, 464, 486, 487, 504, 526, 571, 690, 707, 716, 717, 757, 769, 820, 837, 847, 848, 849, 881, 886, 928, 950, 958].

913 _____. "To the End of the Earth: Acts 1:8," *ET* 89 (1978): 374-75 [*see also* 006, 042, 064, 076, 078, 084, 100, 126, 128, 148, 189, 195, 196, 277, 309, 312, 315, 319, 320, 322, 327, 371, 372, 387, 403, 439, 459, 462, 475, 482, 519, 522, 528, 532, 541, 549, 574, 586, 590, 609, 611, 614, 623, 632, 643, 692, 699, 709, 737, 755, 759, 772, 783, 784, 808, 817, 830, 864, 867, 872, 891, 894, 898, 900, 917, 919, 934, 939, 944, 960, 964, 974].

914 Thurston, B. B. "τὸ ὑπερῷον in Acts 1,13," *ET* 81/1 (1968): 21-22 [*see also* 057, 059, 461, 689, 885].

915 Thurston, R. W. " 'Midrash' and 'Magne' Words in the NT," *EQ* 51 (1979): 22-39 [*see also* 233, 567].

916 Tiede, D. L. "Acts 1:6-8 and the Theo-Political Claims of Christian Witness," *WWo* 1/1 (1981): 41-51 [*see also* 368, 585].

917 _____. "Acts 2:1-47," *Int* 33 (1979): 62-67 [*see also* 006, 042, 064, 076, 078, 084, 100, 126, 128, 148, 189, 195, 196, 277, 309, 312, 315, 319, 320, 322, 327, 371, 372, 387, 403, 439, 459, 462, 475, 482, 519, 522, 528, 532, 541, 549, 574, 586, 590, 609, 611, 614, 623, 632, 643, 692, 699, 709, 737, 755, 759, 772, 783, 784, 808, 817, 830, 864, 867, 872, 891, 894, 898, 900, 913, 917, 934, 939, 944, 960, 964, 974].

918 Tissot, Y. "Les prescriptions des presbytres (Actes 15,41,D). Exégèse et origine du décret dans le texte syro-occidental des *Actes*," *RB* 77/3 (1970): 321-46.

919 Tolbert, M. O. "Contemporary Issues in the Book of Acts," *REx* 71/4 (1974): 521-31 [*see also* 258, 268, 294, 318, 319, 383, 402, 593, 941].

920 Tom, W. "Vervuld met de Heilige Geest. Norm of uitzondering?" *GTT* 61 (1961): 74-76.

921 Townsend, J. T. "The Speeches in Acts," *ATR* 42 (1960): 150-59 [*see also* 070, 096, 115, 193, 199, 326, 497, 554, 647, 839, 846, 867, 968].

922 Trémel, Bernard. "La fraction du pain dans les Actes des Apôtres," *LVie* 94 (1969): 76-90.

923 _____. "A propos d'Actes 20,7-12: puissance du thaumaturge ou du témoin?" *RTP* 30/4 (1980): 359-69.

924 _____. "Voie du salut et religion populaire. Paul et Luc face au risque de paganisation," *LV* 30/153-54 (1981): 87-108 [*see also* 088, 390, 436, 451, 467, 674, 700, 868].

925 Trigger, B. G. "La Candace, personnage mysterieus," *Arch* 77 (1974): 10-17.

926 Trites, A. A. "The Importance of Legal Scenes and Language in the Book of Acts," *NT* 16/4 (1974): 278-84 [*see also* 060, 237, 358, 367, 377, 378, 460, 490, 511, 537, 578, 698, 789, 827, 862, 896, 908, 910, 914, 955, 970, 977].

927 Trocmé, Etienne. "L'eglise primitive a la recherche d'elle-meme: Secte chaleureuse ou grande entreprise missionnaire?" *ETR* 54 (1979): 255 [*see also* 003, 021, 133, 296, 308, 355, 445, 512, 551, 569, 632, 703, 777, 801, 810, 897, 928].

928 Trudinger, P. "Stephen and the Life of the Primitive Church," *BibTB* 14/1 (1984): 18-22 [*see also* 003, 021, 133, 296, 308, 355, 445, 512, 551, 569, 632, 703, 777, 801, 810, 897, 927].

929 Trummer, P. "Verstehst du auch, was du liest? (Apg 8,30)," *K* 22 (1980): 103-13.

930 Tschiedel, H. J. "Ein Pfingstwunder im Apollonhymnos (*Hymn. Hom. Ap.* 156-64 und Apg. 2, 1-13)" *ZRGG* 27/1 (1975): 22-39 [*see also* 001, 043, 076, 077, 078, 088, 101, 110, 121, 126, 154, 178, 190, 221, 239, 240, 242, 300, 340, 370, 465, 493, 512, 528, 541, 577, 590, 611, 613, 624, 644, 665, 687, 692, 737, 787, 806, 808, 812, 813, 817, 862, 888, 900, 902, 939, 960, 964, 975].

931 Tudor, Alexandru. "Viata sacramentala a Bisericii in 'Faptele Apostolilor' (Das sakramentale Leben der Kerche in Apg)," *STS* 32/1-2 (1980): 192-210.

932 Tuland, C. G. "The Confusion About Tongues," *ChrTo* 13/5 (1968): 207-209 [*see also* 001, 011, 012, 025, 201, 230, 239, 247, 266, 279, 322, 346, 437, 483, 552, 665, 722, 808, 973, 975].

933 Turbessi, G. "*Quaerere Deum*. Il tema della 'ricerca di Dio' nella S. Scrittura," *RBib* 10/3 (1962): 282-96.

934 Turner, M. M. B. "The Significance of Receiving the Spirit in Luke-Acts: A Survey of Modern Scholarship," *TJ* 2/2 (1981): 131-58 [*see also* 006, 042, 064, 076, 078, 084, 100, 126, 128, 148, 189, 195, 196, 277, 309, 312, 315, 319, 320, 322, 327, 371, 372, 387, 403, 439, 459, 462, 475, 482, 519, 522, 528, 532, 541, 549, 574, 586, 590, 609, 611, 614, 623, 632, 643, 692, 699, 709, 737, 755, 759, 772, 783, 784, 808, 817, 830, 864, 867, 872, 891, 894, 898, 900, 913, 917, 919, 939, 944, 960, 964, 974].

935 Tyson, J. B. "Acts 6:1-7 and Dietary Regulations in Early Christianity," *PRS* 10/2 (1982): 145-61 [*see also* 144, 363, 382, 427, 449, 524, 538, 683, 701, 774, 782, 944, 969].

936 Udick, W. S. "Metanoia as Found in the Acts of the Apostles," *BibTo* 28 (1967): 1943-46.

937 Unger, M. F. "Archaeology and Paul's Tour of Cyprus," *BS* 117/467 (1960): 229-33.

938 _____. "Archaeology and Paul's Visit to Iconium, Lystra, and Derbe," *BS* 118/470 (1961): 107-12 [*see also* 039, 047, 282, 288, 525].

939 _____. "The Significance of Pentecost," *BS* 122/486 (1965): 169-77 [*see also* 006, 042, 064, 076, 078, 084, 100, 126, 128, 148, 189, 195, 196, 277, 309, 312, 315, 319, 320, 322, 327, 371, 372, 387, 403, 439, 459, 462, 475, 482, 519, 522, 528, 532, 541, 549, 574, 586, 590, 609, 611, 614, 623, 632, 643, 692, 699, 709, 737, 755, 759, 772, 783, 784, 808, 817, 830, 864, 867, 872, 891, 894, 898, 900, 913, 917, 919, 934, 944, 960, 964, 974].

940 van Unnik, W. C. "Die Apostelgeschichte und die Häresien," *ZNW* 58/3-4 (1967): 240-46.

941 _____. "The 'Book of Acts'—the Confirmation of the Gospel," *NT* 4/1 (1960): 26-59 [*see also* 258, 268, 294, 318, 319, 383, 402, 593, 919].

942 Vallauri, E. "La filiazione davidica di Gesù negli Atti degli Apostoli," *La* 19/1 (1978): 38-88 [*see also* 013, 106, 448].

943 _____. "La teologia degli Atti," *La* 16/3 (1975): 336-56 [*see also* 129, 527].

944 Valiamangalam, J. "To the End of the Earth," *Bhash* 2/3 (1976): 220-27 [*see also* 006, 042, 064, 076, 078, 084, 100, 126, 128, 148, 189, 195, 196, 277, 309, 312, 315, 319, 320, 322, 327, 371, 372, 387, 403, 439, 459, 462, 475, 482, 519, 522, 528, 532, 541, 549, 574, 586, 590, 609, 611, 614, 623, 632, 643, 692, 699, 709, 737, 755, 759, 772, 783, 784, 808, 817, 830, 864, 867, 872, 891, 894, 898, 900, 913, 917, 919, 934, 939, 960, 964, 974].

945 Veillé, Monique. "Écriture et prédication: Actes 16,16-24" *ETR* 54/2 (1979): 271-78.

946 Veltman, Fred. "The Defense Speeches of Paul in Acts," *PRS* 5 (1978): 243-56.

947 del Verme, M. "La communione dei beni nella comunita primitiva de Gerusalemme," *RBib* 23/4 (1975): 353-82 [*see also* 194, 430, 479, 835].

948 _____. "Comunione e condivisione dei beni. Chiesa primitiva I e giudaismo esseno-qumranico a confromto," *RQ* 10 (1979): 119.

949 Vesco, J. L. "Le troisième voyage de Paul en Asie Mineure," *BTS* 144 (1972): 6-20 [*see also* 047, 069, 151, 155, 156, 163, 166, 280, 329, 476, 615, 841, 984].

950 Via, J. "An Interpretation of Acts 7,35-37 from the Perspective of Major Themes in Luke-Acts," *PRS* 6/3 (1979): 190-207 [*see also* 024, 055, 058, 077, 142, 168, 223, 334, 343, 363, 386, 458, 462, 506, 508, 609, 675, 678, 683, 756, 763, 803, 832, 862].

951 Vööbus, A. "Die Entdeckung von Überresten der altsyrischen Apostelgeschichte," *OCh* 64 (1980): 32-35.

952 Voss, Gerhard. "Durch die Rechte Gottes erhöt, hat er den Geist ausgegossen (Apg 2,33). Pfingstgeschehen und Pfingstbotschaft nach Apostelgeschichte Kap. 2," *BiKi* 21/2 (1966): 45-47 [*see also* 120, 342, 453, 518, 619, 852].

953 _____. " 'Zum Herrn und Messias gemacht hat Gott diesen Jesus' (Apg 2,36). Zur Christologie der lukanischen Schriften," *BiKi* 8/4 (1967): 236-48 [*see also* 010, 016, 374, 423, 466, 482, 488, 502, 533, 555, 581, 626, 629, 677, 792, 863, 900].

954 Vouga, Francois. "Paul face aux églises de son temps," *LVie* 139 (1978): 21-29.

955 de Waard, Jan. "The Quotation from Deuteronomy in Acts 3,22.23 and the Palestinian Text: Additional Arguments," *Bib* 52/4 (1971): 537-40 [*see also* 060, 237, 358, 367, 377, 378, 460, 490, 511, 537, 578, 698, 789, 827, 862, 896, 908, 910, 914, 926, 970, 977].

956 Wainwright, A. W. "The Historical Value of Acts 9:19b-30," *TU* 112/6 (1973): 589-94.

957 Walker, W. O. "The Timothy-Titus Problem Reconsidered," *ET* 92/8 (1981): 231-35.

958 Walter, N. "Apostelgeschichte 6.1 und die Anfänge der Urge-meinde in Jerusalem," *NTS* 29/3 (1983): 370-93 [*see also* 254, 397, 526, 703, 710, 728, 736].

959 Walvoord, J. F. "The Ascension of Christ," *BS* 121/481 (1964): 2-12 [*see also* 055, 154, 175, 207, 210, 269, 274, 335, 368, 369, 462, 506, 508, 531, 536, 539, 540, 612, 614, 793, 827, 977].

960 Wansbrough, H. W. "The Coming of the Spirit," *CRev* 54/5 (1969): 357-61 [*see also* 006, 042, 064, 076, 078, 084, 100, 126, 128, 148, 189, 195, 196, 277, 309, 312, 315, 319, 320, 322, 327, 371, 372, 387, 403, 439, 459, 462, 475, 482, 519, 522, 528, 532, 541, 549, 574, 586, 590, 609, 611, 614, 623, 632, 643, 692, 699, 709, 737, 755, 759, 772, 783, 784, 808, 817, 830, 864, 867, 872, 891, 894, 898, 900, 913, 917, 919, 934, 939, 944, 964, 974].

961 Weiser, Alfons. "Die Gerichtsgleichnisse in der Verkundigung Jesu," *BiKi* 2 (1978): 48-52 [*see also* 136, 149, 200, 295, 359, 518, 522, 538, 558, 591, 646, 683, 703, 848, 905].

962 ──────. "Das Gottesurteil über Hananias und Saphira; Apg 5,1-11" *TGl* 69/2 (1979): 148-58 [*see also* 102, 172, 549, 611].

963 ──────. "Die Nachwahl des Mattias (Apg 1,15-26). Zur Re-zeption und Deutung urchristlicher Geschichte durch Lu-kas," *QD* 87 (1979): 97-110 [*see also* 038, 187, 278, 425, 537, 654, 787, 970].

964 ──────. "Die Pfingstpredigt des Lukas," *BibLeb* 14/1 (1973): 1-12 [*see also* 006, 042, 064, 076, 078, 084, 100, 126, 128, 148, 189, 195, 196, 277, 309, 312, 315, 319, 320, 322, 327, 371, 372, 387, 403, 439, 459, 462, 475, 482, 519, 522, 528, 532, 541, 549, 574, 586, 590, 609, 611, 614, 623, 632, 643, 692, 699, 709, 737, 755, 759, 772, 783, 784, 808, 817, 830, 864, 867, 872, 891, 894, 898, 900, 913, 917, 919, 934, 939, 944, 960, 974].

965 Wenham, J. "Did Peter Go to Rome in A.D. 42?" *TB* 23 (1972): 94-102 [*see also* 050, 107, 162, 176, 181, 219, 245, 250, 252, 328, 414, 498, 640, 645, 658, 672, 711, 785, 787, 815, 942, 964].

966 _____. "The Theology of Unclean Food," *EQ* 53/1 (1981): 6-15.

967 Wilckens, U. "Die Missionsreden der Apostelgeschichte," *WM* 5 (1974): 56.

968 Wilcox, M. "A Foreword to the Study of the Speeches in Acts," *SJLA* 12/1 (1975): 206-25 [*see also* 070, 096, 115, 193, 199, 326, 497, 554, 647, 839, 846, 867, 921].

969 _____. "The 'God-Fearers' in Acts: A Reconsideration," *JSNT* 13 (1981): 102-22 [*see also* 144, 363, 382, 427, 449, 524, 538, 683, 701, 774, 782, 935, 944].

970 _____. "The Judas-Tradition in Acts i. 15-26," *NTS* 19/4 (1973): 438-52 [*see also* 038, 187, 278, 425, 537, 654, 787, 963].

971 Wilkinson, J. "Jewish Influences on the Early Christian Rite of Jerusalem," *Mu* 92 (1978): 347-59 [*see also* 035, 100, 148, 167, 178, 232, 323, 372, 503, 504, 564, 609, 661, 739, 760, 777, 784, 812, 850, 854, 869, 870, 890, 895, 941, 984, 987].

972 Wilkinson, T. L. "Acts 17: The Gospel Related to Paganism. Contemporary Relevance," *VR* 35 (1980): 1-14 [*see also* 192, 193, 382, 429].

973 _____. "Tongues and Prophecy in Acts and 1st Corinthians," *VR* 31 (1978): 1-20 [*see also* 438].

974 _____. "Two-Stage Christianity: Baptism with the Holy Spirit (...Acts 2,37ss;8,4.24; 10,22; 19,1ss)," *VR* 21 (1973): 1-21 [*see also* 152, 196, 270, 315, 324, 448, 488, 603, 673, 699, 817, 907].

975 Williams, C. G. "Glossolalia as a Religious Phenomenon: 'Tongues' at Corinth and Pentecost," *Rel* 5/1 (1975): 16-32 [*see also* 156, 184].

976 Williams, R. B. "Reflections on the Transmission of Tradition in the Early Church," *En* 40 (1979): 273-85.

977 Wilson, S. G. "The Ascension: A Critique and an Interpretation," *ZNW* 59 (1968): 269-81 [*see also* 055, 154, 175, 207, 210, 269, 274, 335, 368, 369, 462, 506, 508, 531, 536, 539, 540, 612, 614, 793, 827, 959].

978 Witherington, B. "The Anti-Feminist Tendencies of the 'Western' Text in Acts," *JBL* 103/1 (1984): 82-84 [*see also* 367, 576, 719, 908].

979 Wood, J. E. "Isaac Typology in the New Testament," *NTS* 14 (1968): 583-89.

980 Wycherley, R. E. "St. Paul at Athens," *JTS* 9/2 (1968): 619-21 [*see also* 017, 020, 086, 091, 132, 276, 394, 509, 604, 635, 680, 725, 852].

981 Yaure, L. "Elymas—Nehelamite—Pethor," *JBL* 79/4 (1960): 297-314 [*see also* 008, 146, 249].

982 Young, J. E. "That Some Should Be Apostles (Acts 1,21-22)," *EQ* 48 (1976): 96-104.

983 Zeilinger, F. "Lukas, Anwalt des Paulus. Überlegungen zur Abschiedsrede von Milet Apg 20,18-35," *BiLi* 54/3 (1981): 167-72.

984 Zeitlin, S. "Paul's Journeys to Jerusalem," *JQR* 57 (1967): 171-78 [*see also* 035, 100, 148, 167, 178, 232, 323, 372, 503, 504, 564, 609, 661, 739, 760, 777, 784, 812, 850, 854, 869, 870, 890, 895, 941, 971, 987].

985 _____. "Who Were the Galileans? New Light on Josephus' Activities in Galilee," *JQR* 64 (1974): 189-203 [*see also* 169, 578].

986 Ziesler, J. A. "The Name of Jesus in the Acts of the Apostles," *JSNT* 4 (1979): 28-41.

987 Zimmermann, H. "Die Sammelberichte der Apostelgeschichte," *BZ* 5/1 (1961): 71-82 [*see also* 035, 100, 148, 167, 178, 232, 323, 372, 503, 504, 564, 609, 661, 739, 760, 777, 784, 812, 850, 854, 869, 870, 890, 895, 941, 971, 984].

988 _____. "To This Agree the Words of the Prophets (Acts 15,14-17)," *GTJ* 4 (1963): 28-40.

989 Zón, A. "Ekleziologiczny sens terminus 'Droga' w Dz 9, 2," *RBL* 17/4 (1964): 207-15.

990 Zovkic, M. "Krscani kao obraceni gospodinu (Dj. Ap. 9,32-35; 11,19-21) Christiani tamquan conversi ad Cominum in Acts 9,32-35; 11,19-21," *BogS* 44 (1974): 507-23.

991 Zumstein, J. ''L'apôtre comme martyr dans les Actes de Luc. Essai de lecture globale,'' *RTP* 30/4 (1980): 371-90.

Journal Index

Scripture Index

Subject Index

Nicolaitans, 079

Old Latin Text, 909
Old Syriac Text, 460
Old Testament, use in early church, 287, 507
Ordination, 183, 316

Paganism, 192, 193, 382, 429, 972
Palestine, geography of, 396
Parousia, 138, 402
Parrēsia, 128
Parthians, 472
Passion of Christ, 442
Paul, 044, 089, 180, 252, 288, 645, 653, 661, 708, 795, 815, 877, 893, 942, 980; appeal to Emperor, 124; appeal to historical evidence, 572; charges against, 314; chronology of, 361; conversion of, 389, 457, 516, 607, 804, 882; defense of, 458, 677; escape of, 607; journeys of, 047, 069, 151, 155, 156, 163, 166, 280, 329, 476, 615, 841, 949, 984; last days of, 816; life of, 027, 063, 112, 138, 282; letters of (prologues), 145; literature on, 095; preaching of, 405, 794; speeches of, 086, 091, 098, 217, 218, 243, 431, 432, 554, 678, 725, 852; as tentmaker, 404; as theological authority, 411; trial of, 027, 103; trip to Rome, 004, 005, 118, 392, 669, 501, 734; vision of, 053
Paulinisms, 543, 641
Paulus Alexandrinus, 073
Pentecost, 001, 043, 076, 077, 078, 088, 101, 110, 121, 126, 154, 178, 190, 221, 239, 240, 242, 300, 340, 370, 465, 493, 512, 528, 541, 577, 590, 611, 613, 624, 644, 665, 687, 692, 737, 787, 806, 808, 812, 813, 817, 862, 888, 900, 902, 930, 939, 960, 964, 975
Persecution, 710
Peter, 050, 107, 162, 176, 181, 219, 245, 250, 252, 328, 414, 498, 640, 645, 658, 672, 711, 785, 787, 815, 942, 964, 965; preaching of, 030, 216, 234, 240, 465, 560; vision of, 360, 415
Pharisees, 500
Philip, 037, 063, 109, 174, 208, 270, 602, 603, 681, 690, 800

Philippi, 760
Phrygia, 391, 395
Physical healing, 265
Pilate, 180, 471
Pisidian Antioch, 431
Plato, 730
Plutarch, 578
Polybius, 578
Prayer, 864, 911
Preaching, 324
Pre-Pauline Christianity, 834
Preface of Acts, 696
Presbyters, 918
Priscilla, 855
Prologue, of Acts, 157
Prophets, in the New Testament, 438, 973; gift of, 790
Proselyte instruction, 510
Psalms, 222
Pseudo-Clementines, 480

Qumran, 038, 146, 233, 255, 262, 420, 513, 597, 804, 805, 947

Rebaptism, 700
Redactional studies, 464
Redaction criticism, 068
Repentance, 196, 401, 817, 865, 906
Resurrection, 024, 055, 058, 077, 142, 168, 223, 334, 343, 363, 386, 458, 462, 506, 508, 609, 675, 678, 683, 756, 763, 803, 832, 862, 950
Riot at Ephesus, 467
Rites, early Christian, 971
Roman citizenship, rights of, 761
Roman law, 052
Romances, ancient, 825
Rome, 323, 472, 564, 598, 694, 735, 741, 784, 825, 869, 941, 965; church at, 446

Sacrament, 931
Sadducees, 024, 500
Sahidic text, 490
Salvation, 055, 226, 227, 320, 644, 647
Samaria, 736, 837
Samaritan, Christianity, 845; Pentateuch, 745, 766
Samaritanism, 600
Samaritans, 122, 129
Sanhedrin, 057, 059, 461, 689, 885, 914